WOMEN OF COLOR AND FEMINISM

Women of Color and Feminism

Published by
Seal Press
A Member of the Perseus Books Group
1700 Fourth Street
Berkeley, California

Library of Congress Cataloging-in-Publication Data

Rojas, Maythee.
  Women of color and feminism / Maythee Rojas.
  p. cm. -- (Seal studies)
  Includes bibliographical references and index.
  ISBN 978-1-58005-272-6
  1. Women minorities. 2. Feminism. I. Title.
  HQ1161.R65 2009
  305.48'8--dc22
          2009033866

Cover design by Kate Basart, Union Pageworks
Cover illustration © Lauren Simkin Berke c/o rileyillustration.com
Interior design by Michael Walters
Printed in the United States of America by Maple-Vail
Distributed by Publishers Group West

WOMEN OF COLOR AND FEMINISM

MAYTHEE ROJAS, PhD

To my friend and former student,
Roxana Rivera (1977–2003)

CONTENTS

PROLOGUE

IN HER BOOK *THE COLOR OF JEWS* Melanie Kaye/Kantrowitz shares an anecdote that I find particularly helpful in explaining why a book about women of color should be essential reading for everyone. Regularly teaching courses on topics such as racism, poverty, and anti-Semitism, she describes the inevitable moment when a student who has grown weary of discussing these issues raises her hand and asks, "Can't we just be people?" Kaye/Kantrowitz's response is blunt: "That's what racism [or any other oppression] costs you. . . . You don't get to just be a person." What she means is that social injustice—whether we cause it, are hurt by it, or happen to benefit from its effects—dehumanizes all of us. Our constructed identities serve only to protect us from or expose us to oppression in different ways. Saying we do not support racism or sexism does not absolve us from the harm that these discriminations cause others. In fact, unless we actively disrupt the system daily and in radical ways, we can all become accomplices to oppression. Consequently, whether we choose to recognize it or not, at different times all of us give up the right to be considered "just people" as long as social injustice and inequality prevail. In the meantime, we must get in line with everyone else and pick up the baggage that comes with the category or identity that we have (usually unconsciously) agreed to assume.

In my own discussions with students, I like to tell them that no one leaps out of the womb claiming to be an oppressor. Yet from the moment we are born, opportunities and disadvantages are laid out based on our race/ethnicity, gender, class, and sexuality. When we choose not to critically analyze who we are or the paths that have gotten us to where we are today, we become less than whole. In particular, we relinquish part of our humanity because this process dissociates us from other human beings. We learn to forget that our actions are tied to the lives of others. In turn, others grow up suspicious of us because of what they learn to associate with the identities that we take on. As Kaye/Kantrowitz aptly puts it, "Mistrust poisons the air."

If you do not identify as a woman of color, you might not initially see the point of picking up this book, but I urge you to read on. If you are a woman of color, I ask you to consider how your life histories are interconnected with someone else's. How much do any of us really know about each other's cultural pasts? In a wonderful essay about storytelling and the origins of our world, John Edgar Wideman writes, "Suddenly, the mist cleared. Below the people, the earth had changed. It had grown into the shape of the stories they'd told—a shape as wondrous and new and real as the words they'd spoken. But it was also a world unfinished, because not all the stories had been told." This is how I imagine that learning about the lives and experiences of women of color can change everyone's world and improve our individual lives. We have stories to hear that will in turn prompt us to share our own. We have stories to revisit because some aspects were previously left out. We have stories to go back and find before they are permanently lost, and we have stories we altogether need to forget. In short, we have a lot of talking and sharing to do.

This exchange can take place, however, only when we switch up the standard order in which we are used to receiving information. It's what we in academia tend to call "decentering." The "centers" of our society—the dominant stories that our culture tells—are so embedded in our minds that we take them as absolutes and have a hard time thinking around them without some external push to remind us that when we shift our perspective, we gain a whole new set of insights. In fact, amassing as much knowledge as we can about the world (and subsequently ourselves) should be ultimately one of our lifetime goals. It moves us toward wholeness, toward enlightenment. While we may never get there completely, it is the process of trying that becomes our self-realization.

Part of the project of feminism has been to put women's stories at the center, to understand the world through the perspective of women. But often the generic "women" has meant white women. Consequently, feminism has not always been embraced by women of color, even those who in all other ways are already politicized individuals. As the chapters of this book will illustrate, there are many reasons for this alienation. I believe that this disjuncture is not irreparable; however, it does require some pause.

Every day it seems I am confronted with the dilemma of whether or not to publicly acknowledge that I am a feminist. The choice would appear easy enough given that I teach in a women's studies department. However, as a Latina from a working-class background whose family and friends are still largely removed from the academic world, I often feel the tension that the word raises when it is brought up. Truthfully, it can be difficult enough just admitting I have a doctorate. When I share this struggle with my students, most of them readily confess to the same problem. Attending a highly diverse, working-class commuter campus, many of them are the first in their families to attend college. Or they are returning to school and have families at home that demand much of their attention. The intellectual work that they do at school frequently does not have a place in their lives outside of the campus. To introduce labels such as "feminist" into their day-to-day conversations, several admit, is just asking for trouble.

Similarly, the concept "women of color" is also one that raises questions for people. Most of my female students do not walk in thinking of themselves as women of color even though many identify as being part of a certain ethnicity, such as Peruvian or Vietnamese. Others tend to adopt a broader term such as "Latina" or "African American." Again, there are several reasons why this may be the case, some of which are addressed in subsequent chapters. However, it is worth recognizing the general lack of exposure that people—even students—have to the term before entering a class such as mine. They initially share the same blank look I get whenever I mention the term "woman of color" to someone in passing. Why is this term not used more widely, *at least* within the university system? The blank looks I receive when I use the term appear to point perhaps to the greater lack of attention given to the experiences and lives of women of color.

Literary scholar Rachel Lee argues that the marginalization of women of color within the field of women's studies and the greater university structure is at least partially to blame. She describes how at her university the only course to collectively address women of color is set up to meet diversity requirements both within and outside the women's studies major. Thus, it attracts students who have never been exposed to the issues raised, and it can leave them feeling as though the course is only a tacked-on attempt at political correctness and fulfills all that they will ever need to know about this subject matter. Students can then continue with the rest of their educations without ever returning to the issues addressed in the course.

Similarly, a singular course on women of color can marginalize the person teaching it. In particular, it depends on the instructor's physical "body" to authenticate the course (and the department and university), as Lee argues. Ironically, she also notes, this process can distort the instructor's actual identity with a constructed one. Instead of being a Latina scholar of American literature (as I am) or "an Asian American woman, an interpreter of literature, or even a professor of Women's Studies" (as Lee describes herself), as professors who happen to be women of color, we are sometimes thrust into the role of teaching classes on women of color simply because of our perceived identities.

In fact, while incorporating women of color in the curriculum can present the opportunity to expose a great many people to new ideas, it is very difficult as an instructor to have to start from scratch with students and discuss topics and histories that are so complex and extensive within such a brief period as a semester or school quarter. The same might be said of a single book on the topic. The task of trying to provide readers an overview of how feminism and the issues facing women of color intersect has been a tremendous challenge to me. Narrowing down what to include as well as *whom* to talk about was overwhelmingly difficult. Ultimately, I decided to focus largely on the four major ethnic groups recognized in the United States (i.e., Native American, African American, Chicana/o and Latina/o, and Asian American), but this decision has never been an entirely satisfying one. So many other ethnic communities in the United States have had significant experiences here, and they share cross-cultural ties both with each other and with the groups I discuss. At the same time, I could not find room in the book for some of the important issues facing the communities that I do discuss.

Understandably, this book is meant to be only an introduction to and overview of the subject of women of color and feminism. I hope that you, reader, whoever you are, will find it informative, useful, and moving. More important, I hope that you will be encouraged to learn more about the people, issues, and communities mentioned as well as find yourself curious enough to investigate those that I could not fit into this book. In other words, I hope that you will in fact view this as only an introduction to what can become a lifetime of learning about your fellow sisters and brothers of the world. They have many, many stories to feed us and reshape how we think about the world.

CHAPTER 1

DEFINING IDENTITIES

LAST SUMMER, I SPENT TWO WEEKS caring for my sister and brother-in-law's young daughter while they vacationed. Although I experienced a number of new things with my niece, Annika, the most unexpected one occurred when we visited a local park. While we were playing in the sandbox, a little boy and his mother approached us. The boy seemed eager to join my niece. His mother, however, appeared less enthusiastic. She prodded him to keep moving. In an attempt to be friendly, I asked her what his name was. She answered, "Fernando," and then disapprovingly added, "*Todos los negritos quieren las güeritas. Todos son igual.*" Unsure of how to reply, I just gave her a sheepish grin and let them walk away. Despite the fact that I spend most of my days discussing issues of race and gender, I found myself at a loss for words.

"All little black boys want white girls. They are all the same." As a Latina professor of women's studies, I understood what the mother meant. Although Fernando's ethnic origin was unclear, he was dark skinned. Annika is not. The terms *"negra/o"* and *"güera/o"* are frequently used among Latina/os to emphasize differences in skin hues, with preference usually given to those who are lighter. These racialized attitudes about skin tone often determine concepts of beauty and acceptance within the culture. When coupled with the historical prohibitions against interactions between black (and other dark-skinned) men and white women, Fernando's interest in my light-skinned niece likely appeared suspicious to his mother. Viewing her son's intention through the prism

1

of racialized desire, she probably assumed her son would not escape its legacy. Intellectually, I understood all of this. However, emotionally, her words left me pained. Why couldn't Fernando's interest just be childhood curiosity? What about the fact that Annika *is* Latina?

A short time later, the park started to clear out and my niece and I made our way back to our car. Next to us, another Latino family was packing up, and their young son sat waiting in his stroller. I pointed at him and spoke to my niece in Spanish. His father stared at us for a moment and then hesitantly asked if she were my daughter. After I explained she was actually my niece, his facial expression left me feeling that he was unconvinced, so I reassuringly added that I recognized how *güerita* she looked. He nodded with a quick smile and turned back to his family. However, as I drove away, I became upset. Within one brief outing, both my niece and I had been misread and our relationship misconstrued. Moreover, I was partially to blame.

My niece is the product of my sister, an olive-toned, dark-featured American of Costa Rican descent, and her husband, a blond, green-eyed American of mixed European descent. Most agree that Annika is a good combination of the two; however, I regularly see my sister in her, especially given Annika's dark eyes. It had never crossed my mind that we might not look related. I also never considered that others might assume she was not Latina. Regularly surrounded by our side of the family, she hears Spanish as frequently as English (her first word was "*gracias*"). However, these two encounters, with those I like to think of as my own *gente* (i.e., other Latina/os), reminded me that we often fail to see people's individuality because of the social expectations that we place on them.

During our brief excursion, my niece's particularly light skin and hair color succeeded in darkening my own decisively "ethnic" features in the eyes of those observing us and recast our aunt/niece relationship into the common Latina nanny/white child one that pervades much of Los Angeles. This was why the father in the parking lot seemed confused when I claimed we were related. And this kind of assumption is also what makes the mother's discomfort at her son's interest understandable.

The race and gender dimensions that Annika and Fernando likely faced as playmates are ones long ago established by histories of patriarchy and conquest, both within and outside the United States. These histories shape interactions not only between different ethnic groups, but also between men and women and between different classes. The mother's resentment revealed her understanding (conscious or not) of a set of dialectics, or oppositional power relationships, frequently formed by the intersecting politics of race, class, and gender. In addition, her words underscored the sexual politics that lay trapped in between.

"Identity Is the Bane of Subjectivity's Existence"

Our experience at the park echoes a frustration that Sidonie Smith, a feminist scholar of women's autobiography, has described feeling when trying to make sense of her subjects' lives. In her essay "Identity's Body," she notes that one of the biggest obstacles in accurately writing about her female subjects is that, too often, "identity is the bane of subjectivity's existence." Being able to consciously reflect on our lives and take control of our daily actions allows us to gain subjectivity, but it is easy to lose this sense of control in light of the myriad social identities that typically subsume us. Tied to identities that mark us as belonging to one group or another, each with a set of expected behaviors and actions, we find it difficult to be acknowledged or understood outside of such perimeters. Moreover, when multiple identities are intertwined, it can become nearly impossible to be seen underneath them. We become the Latina nanny. The black boy. The white girl. Each identity carries us along a predestined path where we are met with fixed assumptions, prejudices, and limitations. Ironically, often by the time we reach these moments of misunderstanding, we have absorbed so many of the same messages about ourselves and others that it is unlikely we will resist or challenge them—even when we know better. This is what nagged me the most about the park episode.

Did I make a point of speaking to my niece in Spanish as we were leaving the park in order to emphasize her ethnicity because I was still smarting from the assumption that she was not Latina? At the same time, why did I take up the very same oppressive language that set her apart by calling her a *güerita*? My own responses, as well as those we received, make me wonder what will happen when Annika, born from an ethnically mixed relationship, finds herself drawn to people from other ethnic communities, perhaps also mixed like her. How do we begin to form new conversations?

Examining the women of color whose histories, issues, and individual experiences are central to this book could offer a means of addressing some of these concerns. However, their stories also raise new ones. I teach a course on U.S. women of color and, on the first day of each semester, I routinely ask my students to consider the difficulty of learning about groups as diverse as Asian Americans or Native Americans in the span of one semester. How do we avoid generalizing within and between communities—of race, of class, of gender, and of sexuality? What moves us to identify one group as being "of color" and another not? Where do we start?

In response to these questions, my students often debate the purpose of our class. Some go as far as to claim that they are "over race" and wonder why we have not moved on. We are individuals, not categories, they argue. Besides, they insist, people in the United States no longer care about race. Questions and comments such as these get us talking about the construction of categories, specifically those surrounding race, class, gender, and sexuality. They also get us thinking about how, in our society, we create social hierarchies by ranking according to identity, which then leads to stereotypes and assumptions. Similarly, stereotypes and assumptions generally serve as tools for silencing and oppression. In turn, silence and oppression give way to mechanisms of inequality such as racism and sexism that become entrenched in our daily lives.

Once our conversations take this direction, my students tend to back off from their earlier statements. They remember incidents in which they were affected by what others assumed about them. They admit that they do not know much about other groups' histories, or sometimes their own. They realize that they have lacked words to explain their experiences, and in some cases, were made to believe that they should not matter. Less willing then to uphold the belief that we are past the need for self-examination or that race does not matter, they begin to acknowledge the actual power that naming and identity markers hold and to understand why a class on the topic of women of color is a necessary step to discussing these integral issues. In this case, Smith's observation that "identity is the bane of subjectivity's existence" takes on a more nuanced meaning because recognizing and naming collective experiences can also provide the crucial steps needed to identify key factors of oppression. In other words, to gain autonomy, we often need to first identify struggles in our lives that are actually not about who we are as individuals, but about who we are assumed to be based on our race or class or our gender or sexuality.

Here is one example. In 1975, a class-action civil suit *(Madrigal v. Quilligan)* was filed against the University of Southern California-Los Angeles County Medical Center (LACMC) by a number of women of Mexican origin who had been coercively sterilized while they were patients at the hospital. During a period of at least three years, doctors routinely performed tubal ligations on countless Mexican female patients who were there to give birth. The procedures were done without their consent or the women were forced to sign their approval while they were still in labor. None of the women were fluent in English, and many lacked a thorough understanding of what "tying their tubes" meant.

The issue evolved into a legal matter because Chicana/o activists, hospital employees who recognized the misuse of power, and the women themselves were able to trace how the medical staff systematically treated pregnant female patients of Mexican origin. The common threads were the patients' race, gender, and perceived economic status. The hospital's unethical medical practices might have gone unchecked for much longer if no one had critically analyzed how the bodies and identities of Mexican women were being framed within the greater social context of female reproduction. Court evidence showed that some doctors believed Mexican women were "hyperfertile" and consequently had too many children. Others assumed these women were too poor to afford more children. Acting from their own gender and class status as economically well-to-do men, the doctors justified their abuse by stereotyping their patients. If these women's medical histories had been reviewed solely on an individual basis, they might not have revealed the social factors that contributed to their sterilization. However, their common experience as poor women of color allowed critics to name the oppressive framework that violated them and, in turn, devise a plan of resistance.

While they vary widely in effect, both this grave example and the more innocuous one I experienced in the park illustrate the power of body politics. Bodily differences make identity a two-sided coin: Assumptions based on our physical features or appearances invariably work against our attempts at self-actualization; however, because we are subject to oppressions based on these assumptions, politically claiming certain identities can be our only means to gaining control over our lives.

"A Peculiar Sensation"

In *The Souls of Black Folk*, W. E. B. DuBois argues that African Americans are "gifted with second-sight in this American world, a world which yields him no true self-consciousness, but only lets him see himself through the revelation of the other world. It is a peculiar sensation, this double-consciousness, this sense of always looking at one's self through the eyes of others, of measuring one's soul by the tape of a world that looks on in amused contempt and pity." Although DuBois's discussion singles out the black male experience, the ambivalence he describes is resoundingly poignant for any who experience it. Living as a part of the overall society (i.e., "American") and yet also remaining an outsider to it forces someone to regularly view and judge herself or himself from a marginalized position. At the same time, it positions the dominant group as the norm. It is from this group that the marginalized receive cues about how to behave or fit in. It is also herein where the struggle for subjectivity begins.

In her essay "Not You/Like You: Post-Colonial Women and the Interlocking Questions of Identity and Difference," filmmaker and essayist Trinh T. Minh-ha describes identity as a dividing line that is created between those who have the power to define a person's or group's characteristics and those who are pressured into upholding the dominant group's features despite being expected to embody the opposite of them. She refers to this type of dysfunctional relationship as the "I and not-I." Take, for instance, how men and women are situated in oppositional terms. The pronoun "he" becomes defined and legitimized against everything that "she" is not. This traps men and women in a dualistic relationship and forces those in the "not" category into the position of the Other. If you are not a man, you are other than a man. Neither party fares well in this kind of relationship. Men become fixed to an essence that presumably represents them (e.g., you are a man so you must be tough) and women are either subjected to exist in the shadow of this essence (e.g., you are not a man, so you cannot be tough, but you want to be legitimized so you keep trying to act tough) or they are altogether erased by it (e.g., you are not a man and not tough, so you are destined to invisibility). For those who cannot comfortably or willingly take up either gendered position (e.g., you are queer or transgendered, so popular logic would dictate that there is no way you can ever be tough or, instead, that your toughness makes your gender identity suspect), there is no choice, just erasure. Unless you take a different approach to the concept of difference, that is.

Hegemony, the monster mechanism that holds most forms of oppression in place, works to ensure that we accept binary relationships and buy into the concept of sameness. As feminist theorist Audre Lorde suggests, our many social and state institutions support hegemony by teaching us to strive for uniformity, to see difference as a threat, and to demean or ignore what the majority does not support. In school, that can mean giving preference to one form of writing, one group's history, one type of speech, and one set of ideas. Throughout our legal system, hegemony can make certain inequalities seem just, such as punishing street crimes such as burglary and drug abuse more severely than white-collar crimes such as insider trading or encouraging special tax breaks for corporations but not the average taxpayer. Likewise, cultural outlets such as the media, religion, and even sports can all gear us toward specific notions about what is considered normal or acceptable.

Ever listen to the radio and count how many songs in a row are about heterosexual love? Wonder why there are references to a Christian God in our currency system, our pledge of allegiance, and our Constitution? Why is it usually easier to name ten African American male athletes than it is five politicians? These are just a few examples of how we are socialized to imagine others and ourselves in specific ways. Hegemony operates at both the macrostructural level and the everyday commonplace to support a dominant set of ideologies and practices. Moreover, those who are the most disempowered by hegemonic norms are often the same ones who unknowingly promote them in an attempt to belong. Consider, for instance, the amount of money spent every year to support hegemonic standards of beauty (for example, hair dye, colored contacts, surgical implants, fake tanning) that clearly do not reflect how the majority of people naturally look. Nevertheless, people buy these items in an attempt to transform themselves into who they believe represent ideals of beauty and success. Hegemony convinces them that what they are not is what they should become.

Yet subverting hegemony is not a hopeless prospect. For DuBois, a double consciousness meant forcibly adopting a perspective that left him less than whole. His divided identity kept the hope of being recognized as a fully actualized individual out of reach. He could learn to function within the dominant system, but he was kept from ever escaping its control. However, having a "second sight" also stands to be useful in subverting oppression. The key lies in an active awareness of one's situation and a strategic employment of what makes one different. In *Sister Outsider*, Lorde calls individuals who possess this ability "watchers," those who are "familiar with the language and manners of the oppressor, even sometimes adopting them for some illusion of protection." Sociologist Patricia Hill Collins discovered someone who put it in even plainer terms when she interviewed an African American inner-city resident named Ruth Shays. As Shays concludes, "The mind of the man and the mind of the woman is the same. But this business of living makes women use their minds in ways that men don't even have to think about." Shays's observation is powerful. Her words reveal how individuals live out the everyday complexities of identity. Surviving in a patriarchal society, women learn to respond to a set of social structures that excludes them even as it determines their social roles and expectations. Consequently, they regularly operate within, and therefore understand, two worlds: the conventional, male-centered one and their own world, to which men are not privy.

One student with whom I shared Shays's comment related to it in the following way: She explained that back in the Midwest where she grew up, her father was the family's single wage earner, and in return he expected to have meat at every dinner. It never occurred to him how difficult that might be given their tight budget and large family. Meanwhile, her mother had to regularly figure out where to shop and what type of meat she could afford to get him his meal. The student ruefully recalled how her mother learned the butcher's tricks, which newspapers carried special coupons, and which days the markets slashed their prices. Although the mother's double consciousness did not liberate her from the situation, her forced domestic role did provide her with survival skills that her husband did not possess. More significantly, by watching her, her daughter learned how to name, respond to, and altogether avoid the same experience.

As cultural theorist bell hooks asserts in *Feminist Theory: From Margin to Center*, repositioning difference as a potential weapon of subversion offers the opportunity to shift the line that divides those at society's center from those at its margins and that keeps hegemony lodged in place. It can also force into question the invisible privileges that come with occupying the center position. Specifically, patriarchy and whiteness are both elements in our society that are so ingrained and affixed to our notions of normalcy that they often pass unnoticed.

"White Like Me"

Another question I frequently ask my students during our initial meeting is, why women *of color*? Who exactly does the term describe? Since I teach on a fairly diverse campus, I usually have a few African American female students in class, and they tend to be the first to respond. They admit that when they registered for the course, they assumed it was going to be specifically about them. Upon hearing this, several other students usually nod in agreement. They thought the same thing.

My first year teaching the class, still green from my graduate studies during which I passionately embraced the term "woman of color" as my own, I was surprised by their answer. Then I started to think about it. In drugstores, aisles are set aside for hair and makeup products for women of color. However, these products are usually only for women of African descent. In mainstream bookstores, you can sometimes find books for or about women of color. However, unless they are shelved in a section labeled ETHNIC STUDIES (and sometimes even then, too), the books tend to focus mostly on black women. Or, even when the books do include other groups, they usually feature only black women on the covers. I do not believe this is because black women have some sort of monopoly on the term "women of color" or are in any way overrepresented anywhere else. In fact, it seems quite the opposite.

It is difficult to pinpoint when the term "people of color" entered our American vernacular. Martin Luther King Jr. used the term "citizens of color" in his famous 1963 Lincoln Memorial speech to emphasize the collective experience of oppression faced by different ethnic American communities. Nineteenth-century references to "free people of color" suggest it served as a distinguishing moniker for those freed from slavery. There also may have been earlier usages in which the term described differences in skin pigment related to health issues. However, its increased prominence in the early 1970s and throughout the 1990s brought "people of color" into its current popular usage, making it difficult to ignore race whether you saw the term as empowering or considered it a form of exclusion. Either way, "color" is a word that still evokes a reaction for most Americans, in part perhaps because race is still a largely unexamined concept.

The use of the phrase "of color" in places such as bookshops and drugstores, where my students and much of society are likely to see it, conspicuously highlights the long-standing invisibility of whiteness. Race-identity markers most clearly tell us how certain communities are *not* white. In particular, African Americans and everything else related to black culture become default images whenever the subject of race is broached because, as a nation, our understanding of race is still largely rooted in a black/white polemic derived from African American slavery. Despite our temporal distance from that historical event, we still lack comfort with discussing racism toward African Americans. In our post–civil rights era, whiteness goes partially unexamined because acknowledging race has conveniently become impolite or passé. As Toni Morrison argues in *Playing in the Dark: Whiteness and the Literary Imagination*, "Ignoring race is understood to be a graceful, even generous, liberal gesture. To notice is to recognize an already discredited difference." This may explain why many of my students who grew up learning Spanish cuss words from their Latino friends, bopping to rap music, or trading manga comics think that racism is no longer an issue. In their minds, discussing race just sounds like tiresome diatribe that interferes with their superficial absorption of other cultures.

However, it is precisely the unwillingness to openly address issues of race that keeps the specters of slavery just within reach of our subconscious. Consequently, when inferences to race such as the phrase "of color" are injected into everyday life, our imaginations revert to images of a constructed blackness and a history in which "colored" meant being African American. Ironically, though, few Americans actually understand what makes up that history. The end of slavery gave way to many other forms of prejudice, separatism, and violence. Among them was the "one-drop" rule, which held that a person with

Black People Love Us!

Is it okay to joke about race? Does it depend on who is telling the jokes? Can stereotypes ever be humorous? These are just some of the questions raised by the satirical website www.blackpeopleloveus.com. When viewers visit the site, they are met by a smiling, rather blank-eyed white couple named Sally and Johnny and a series of pictures featuring them socializing with their "black friends." On the webpage, the couple brag about how much the black community likes them and how unique that is "since lots of Black people don't like lots of White people." To prove their point, they include testimonials from these "friends" that describe what makes Sally and Johnny so great. One friend notes, "Sally always says things that make me feel special, like: 'You're so cool, you're different, you're not like other Black people!'" Another remarks, "Johnny always says: 'I'm not racist; one of my best friends is Black!' I think he might mean me!" On subsequent pages, the website features Sally and Johnny playing games such as Pictionary and hangman in which the couple's cluelessness about African Americans and the issue of racism becomes obvious. This is one of the ways in which this somewhat controversial website offers itself as a teaching tool on race matters. As the *New York Times* puts it, the site provides "a form of social activism, a way of examining the infinitely complex subject of race relations."

Yet viewers stumbling onto this website are often confused. Most wonder, *Is this site for real?* Many are appalled. In the section marked YOUR LETTERS, visitors leave notes that vary from supportive to outraged. Several find the approach to discussing race refreshing. They describe how the guise of a friendship often allows people to assume they can say inappropriate things. Similarly, some visitors note the widespread ignorance that continues to exist because people somehow believe that knowing someone black automatically absolves them of racism. Many of the messages are from African Americans who relate to hearing Sally and Johnny's clueless comments and share other indignations they have had to suffer with coworkers, friends, and strangers. For example, one African American student with self-described "nappy-ass hair" writes, "I swear, if one more white person says that they want to touch my hair, I am gonna put a f*ckin mousetrap in it so their f*ckin hand gets caught in it." Another message commends the site for bringing all types of stereotypes to bear by portraying Sally and Johnny as typical whites who are into "golf, horseback riding, arts and crafts, gardening, [and] building treehouses." Still, others do not think the website is clear enough in its purpose. Some think its creators do more harm than good by "perpetuat[ing] the very problem they are attempting to critique." More than one visitor believes the approach is immature and ineffective.

Black People Love Us! went up in 2002 and during its first month received six hundred thousand visitors. Its creators, brother-and-sister team Jonah and Chelsea Peretti, explain that they set the site up to encourage a discourse around race. In particular, they wanted to gear the discussion toward a white audience. "I think it's important that white people think about race," Jonah told the Boston Herald. "If only people of color can talk about race, there's this division of labor where white people don't have to worry about racism, and it's out of sight, out of mind."

The Perettis grew up in the diverse city of Oakland, California. In addition to their having their own "black friends," their father married a black woman after divorcing their mother and the siblings grew up sharing a close relationship with her. They often noted how differently their stepmother was treated and learned to consider race issues through her perspective. This was one reason they decided to omit the creators' race from the site. As Chelsea explains in her interview with the New York Times, "Part of the purpose of the site is to have people think about what is this and why it exists and not who is behind it." In fact, curiosity about the website's creators is part of what keeps the dialogue going. Some visitors argue that the satire's validity depends on the creators' race; others commend the use of self-deprecating humor to broach a touchy subject. In either case, the crowd of daily visitors and messages to the site indicate that race remains a relevant issue to discuss.

any trace of African ancestry could not be considered white and would be classified as colored. In conjunction with antimiscegenation laws, this ideology was written into legislation that most states adopted to prevent interracial marriage and ensure a permanent status of inequality based on race. In turn, these actions encouraged whoever was able to hide his or her heritage and whenever possible to pass for white. This not only included African Americans, but also Asians, Native Americans, and Latinos, who were also heavily ostracized by white society and who still remain largely invisible when issues of race are raised. "Passing" relied on the power of visual markers to convince people that what they thought they saw was what they were expecting to see (in other words, if someone looked white, she *must* be white). As an act of resistance, however, passing became a means of both avoiding oppression and gaining access to privileges normally reserved for whites.

Discussing white privilege is usually another thorny area for people. While most folks are genuinely disturbed by outward acts of racism (a racially motivated beating or a cross burned on someone's lawn, for instance), few can readily acknowledge the ways in which they benefit from the effects of racism. In fact, this tends to be where alliances are most often tested. It can be very difficult for individuals to reconcile their desire for a just society with the realization that there are numerous comforts that they receive and would have to give up if racism ceased to exist.

In 1990, Wellesley College professor Peggy McIntosh created a list of advantages she held as a white person in the United States. The list, which numbered fifty items, was accompanied by a brief essay in which McIntosh referred to white privilege as "an invisible weightless knapsack of special provisions, maps, passports, codebooks, visas, clothes, tools, and blank checks." This metaphor emphasizes the bundle of shortcuts that those fitting what Lorde calls the "mythical norm" automatically receive with their daily membership in the United States. As Lorde explains in *Sister Outsider*, "In America, this norm is usually defined as white, thin, male, young, heterosexual, Christian, and financially secure. It is with this mythical norm that the trappings of power reside within society." Lorde's profile of the power brokers in our culture is echoed in McIntosh's list of admitted advantages. Here are just a few of her examples that illustrate the depth of ease and self-confidence attached to whiteness:

> *#13: Whether I use checks, credit cards or cash, I can count on my skin color not to work against the appearance of financial reliability.*
>
> *#23: I can criticize our government and talk about how much I fear its policies and behavior without being seen as a cultural outsider.*
>
> *#46: I can choose blemish cover or bandages in "flesh" color and have them more or less match my skin.*

Individuals who never suffer the stigmas attached to race and ethnicity usually take white privilege for granted. In fact, as McIntosh notes, because they experience the ability to readily act and move about in society, many white Americans come to define their lives as "morally neutral, normative, and average, and also ideal." Consequently, proponents of assimilation in the United States believe that, with the right conditioning, others can live the same. However, this argument ignores the fact that the process by which individuals adapt to the dominant culture requires that difference be viewed negatively. Assimilation teaches that difference is bad. Moreover, it enforces disparity by setting up barriers to those who do not or cannot conform. Not assimilating becomes a punishment. Thus, the reality is that you cannot enjoy the promises of assimilation without supporting the oppression of others. In more basic terms, whiteness can be understood as that ticket that earns someone a seat away from the back of the bus. It is really a form of collateral.

Comedian Eddie Murphy capitalized on the humor of exploring white privilege in a sketch that aired December 15, 1984, on the satirical television show *Saturday Night Live*. "White Like Me" featured Murphy in an undercover operation to "experience America

. . . as a white man." Wearing makeup and a wig and donning a suit and tie to reflect a business professional, Murphy set out to discover if there were in fact "two Americas: one black and one white." Through a series of encounters with white people, the camera followed him as he attempted to buy a newspaper, apply for a loan, and take a bus ride. In each case, he reaped the benefits of his white appearance by realizing "when white people are alone, they give things to each other for free." Murphy relied on exaggerated circumstances to engage viewers. He also poked fun at stereotypes that included white mainstream culture by claiming he prepared for his role by watching episodes of *Dynasty* and reading Hallmark cards. However, Murphy's message was unmistakably political in his closing comments: "So, what did I learn from all of this? Well, I learned that we still have a very long way to go in this country before all men are truly equal. But I'll tell you something. I've got a lot of friends, and we've got a lot of makeup. So, the next time you're huggin' up with some really super, groovy white guy, or you met a really great, superkeen white chick, don't be too sure. They might be black."

Identity Nations

In the late 1960s and early 1970s, after the activism of the civil rights era, umbrella nationalist liberation groups such as the American Indian Movement (AIM), the Chicano Movement, the Asian American Movement, and the Black Power Movement began using skin color as a tool of political empowerment. BLACK IS BEAUTIFUL, BROWN PRIDE, RED POWER, and YELLOW POWER were all slogans that affirmed the concept of cultural unity while highlighting a racial consciousness predicated on the need to improve their communities from within. Additionally, emphasizing race within their political work forced people to notice and question the normative place that whiteness had long held in mainstream culture.

While the activist organizations within these movements varied in agenda and mission, most were made up largely of young men and women who were committed to social change through cultural empowerment.

Chief among their shared concerns were self-determination and economic sovereignty. Through plans, programs, and lists of demands, groups such as the Brown Berets, the Black Panthers, the Red Guard, and Indians of All Tribes spelled out the economic and racial disparities that kept their communities oppressed. To fully realize their place as Americans, they argued, they first required gaining access to a better education, adequate housing, affordable healthcare, and a fair legal system. Using identity markers such as skin color, as well as language and dress, these nationalist groups developed a political strategy to collectively address these issues. In addition, by employing the concept of family as a theme of commonality, they affirmed a commitment to their causes and a loyalty that bound the members to one another.

© Getty Images / Photograph by David Fenton

Two members of the Brown Berets, a Chicano activist group, stand together during a National Chicano Moratorium Committee march in opposition to the war in Vietnam, Los Angeles, California, February 28, 1970.

While the focus on race and culture as unifying factors led some to accuse these nationalist organizations of being separatist or even practicing a reverse form of racism, coalition building was actually common between groups. For example, the Young Lords, which was founded in Chicago and later included chapters in New York, Philadelphia, Boston, and Connecticut, regularly worked with members from the Black Panther Party. In addition, the membership itself was significantly diverse. Although heavily Puerto Rican, the Young Lords counted African Americans, Mexicans, Filipinos, and other ethnic groups among its membership base. Likewise, activists in both AIM and the Chicano Movement shared similar ideological perspectives regarding indigenous rights and commonly engaged in each other's political struggles. In addition, all of these nationalist movements interacted and worked closely with numerous white and Jewish social justice activists. The consciousness-raising era of the 1960s and '70s emphasized how people of various backgrounds had long been working together to address injustices experienced at home and abroad.

One group that significantly illustrates the level of solidarity among multiple nationalist organizations was the Third World Liberation Front (TWLF), a coalition established in 1968 to pressure San Francisco State, initially, and later the University of California, Berkeley to develop Third World Colleges. As historian William Wei notes, the goal was to create academic units that would house different ethnic-specific programs and recruit faculty and staff of color. TWLF wanted to expand the university curricula to directly address the issues facing their communities. The group demanded that the universities offer open admission to students of color and poor, working-class white students, who were greatly underrepresented at the university level. It also argued that conventional course work favored Eurocentric ideologies that marginalized and denied the cultural and historical experiences of third world people.

TWLF's decision to employ the term "third world" in relation to its struggles seems particularly meaningful. As postcolonial scholar Chandra Talpade Mohanty explains, it brings together culturally diverse groups who have experienced similar oppressions as allied "communities of resistance." Although some have argued that using this term can further marginalize by geographically lumping people and countries together, the focus on a shared context of struggle rather than particular color or racial identifications encourages an examination of how economic, social, and cultural factors globally contribute to racial oppression. The TWLF's decision to situate its organizing efforts along worldwide lines demonstrates its conscious attempts at creating cross-cultural alliances.

TWLF staged a series of strikes against the universities, many of which resulted in campus shutdowns and violent clashes with police.

In addition, although the concept of academic freedom should have provided a common foundation of support, academic elitism among the majority of students, faculty, and administrators, particularly at the Berkeley campus, only increased the hostility against the TWLF. Nevertheless, the group received union and community backing and its persistent efforts eventually prevailed as the now-prestigious ethnic studies departments at both campuses attest. In fact, many other universities across the nation have come to view these departments as models for the creation of their own ethnic studies programs and departments.

Conflicting Alliances

While nationalist organizations in the 1970s based their efforts on cultural and political solidarity, their stand on gender and sexuality remained less unified. Women and gays and lesbians were particularly marginalized within nationalist groups. For example, challenges to male chauvinism and homophobia were generally met with accusations of antinationalism and disloyalty. Those who attempted to speak out were regarded as undercover operatives intent on sabotaging the organizations. Others were labeled traitors for challenging sexism and homophobia, which were assumed to be strictly "white people" concerns. In fact, these charges revealed one of the greatest problems with organizing under the ideological concept of "family." Forced to remain loyal to their group's dominant views, those who did not fit the heteronormative, patriarchal dynamic set out by traditional constructions of family were left voiceless. These divisions were further exacerbated by organizations within the women's movement and Gay Liberation Front, which were similarly discriminatory in their interactions with people of color. Overall, being other than male and heterosexual within the various nationalist movements proved to be a polarizing experience for many. To some, it was altogether discouraging. As Chicana lesbian Cherríe Moraga admits in her essay "A Long Line of Vendidas," "No soy tonta [I'm no dummy]. I would have been murdered in El Movimiento—light-skinned, unable to speak Spanish well enough to hang; miserably attracted to women and fighting it; and constantly questioning all authority, including men's. I felt I did not belong there."

Still, many feminist-minded nationalist members did persevere in their challenge to create a just and revolutionary space. For example, in a series of interviews with historian Susie Ling, a number of Asian American women who were activists in the Los Angeles area during the 1960s and '70s expressed experiencing sexual discrimination. They shared the frustration they felt at being relegated to such subordinate tasks as making coffee, answering the phone, cleaning toilets, and handling the mail while the real decision making was left to the male members. The mistreatment also extended to sexual harassment and domestic violence. For instance, after witnessing the continued abuse of one of their fellow activists, a group of women went to the abuser's home and confronted him. Although they intended to "kick his ass" and managed to deliver a few blows, they mostly released the anger they had felt toward him, and toward other men who had disrespected them, by yelling at their male target. The act managed to substantially scare the batterer and it became a moment of empowerment for the women.

Once Asian American female activists became consciously aware of the double standard they faced, many began meeting separately from the men and addressing issues that pertained specifically to them. In Los Angeles, a women's collective created childcare centers, held drug intervention programs for Asian American female youth, and developed international ties with their Asian sisters in other countries. They also held self-improvement workshops where they discussed their emotions and became better educated about international issues. Yet throughout their endeavors, the women never advocated joining the women's movement or distancing themselves from the general Asian American activist organizations. As Asian American women, they thought their gender was invariably tied to their race and class, and, consequently, most believed it was more effective to incorporate their issues into the larger context of their community activism. Working separately from their male counterparts was not an option.

For women in the Black Panther Party, the process of reconciling their goals for social justice with the male chauvinism they experienced was less clear. In Sienna McLean's documentary *Still Revolutionaries*, former members Katherine Campbell and Madalynn Carol Rucker discuss the harsh treatment they received within the Black Panther Party despite their devout commitment to the group. Both describe their initial draw to the party's promise of community self-determination and improvement, including a series of social services called "survival programs," such as breakfast for children, clothing and shoe distribution centers, self-defense workshops, free medical clinics, and drug and alcohol rehabilitation programs. However, once immersed in the party, the women soon found that the members' responsibilities were unevenly distributed. Wherever possible, the men avoided childcare responsibilities and other domestic duties, preferring to focus on security detail and physical work instead. More alarmingly, some men sexually harassed the female members, often coercing them into having "sex on demand" based on the argument that it was their duty to abide as revolutionary sisters.

The rank-and-file system the Black Panthers adopted increased the pressure on younger, lower-ranked members by forcing them to acquiesce to unjust demands. This system was also used to deliver corporal punishment. As Elaine Brown, the highest-ranked female Panther, recalls in her memoir, *A Taste of Power*, after being sentenced to ten lashes for failing to get the Black Panther newspaper out on time, "I took the punishment, the way most comrades did. Bobby [Seale]'s order was sufficient. There was no real appeal. It was our judicial system, made up mostly as we went along. . . . Discipline was essential in the vanguard, we told ourselves. So I silently faced the punishment, which was always an act of violence." The culture of fear that developed in response to the extreme use of force, which grew more random as morale deteriorated and the paranoia of betrayal escalated, led many women to eventually abandon the organization. Sadly, they realized, they had become more wary of their comrades than of the police who were considered the main enemy.

At the same time the Panthers were organizing for social justice, many people of Mexican descent who were born or living in the United States adopted the term "Chicano" as a form of protest and cultural pride. Previously, the word had been used derisively among Mexicans and Anglo Americans alike. While its origin is unclear, "Chicano" meant "peasant" in the Nahautl language spoken by the Aztecs, the last reigning indigenous culture before the Spanish conquest. Its pejorative use in contemporary times reflects the deep-rooted racism and classism that many Mexicans, themselves heirs of indigenous communities, have internalized. These feelings of self-loathing have been further exacerbated by the poor and often violent treatment Mexicans have received within the United States.

During the politically charged era of the 1960s and '70s, activists reappropriated the term "Chicano" as a means of addressing multiple oppressions. Being Chicano spoke to their second-class status as U.S. residents and citizens as well as the suppression of their indigenous roots by their own community, which typically favored the idea of a European ancestry. At the same time, the word "Chicano" follows a common practice in the Spanish language: It erases the female presence by encompassing men and women under the suffix "o." Unfortunately, this also carries over into the more sexist traditions of Mexican culture and into several areas of the Chicano movement. Despite playing active, often vital, roles in both, women were frequently discounted and their issues were made secondary or altogether ignored by their supposed *compañeros* in struggle.

Nevertheless, women began bridging the gap between their participation and exclusion in numerous ways. One prime target was to challenge the linguistic sexism of the word "Chicano," a discussion that continues today. Through persistent objections to their exclusion, women have gone from being called Chicano women to Chicanas to introducing the adoption of a/o or o/a as a way of acknowledging both genders when discussing the community. More recently, Chicana/os have also embraced an even more inclusive term: "Chican@." The use of the @ symbol bypasses the need to specify gender or place one ahead of the other. It also opens the term to include members of the transgendered and queer communities. Similarly, as a symbol frequently used in the Internet age, it indicates the still vibrant presence of Chican@ activism. These shifts in language illustrate the possibilities of employing difference as a tool against hegemony. Despite the Chicana/o Movement's commitment to social change, its initial focus on the male experience replicated the white patriarchal culture it was attempting to overthrow. In moving away from using monolithic terms such as "Chicano," the movement more broadly widens its potential impact for the entire community.

Native American women have also counted on their communities' indigenous—and often feminist—roots to combat the sexism perpetuated by Native American men. Before European colonialism, many Indian women held political, economic, and religious power within their tribes. Their roles were usually considered equally important to those of men. However, the introduction of European patriarchy and female subservience into Native American cultures soon changed that. In addition, intermarriages with white men led to a series of detrimental losses for Native women, including their offspring losing clan membership, the loss of tribal property, and a shift in independence as many lost the opportunity to do physical labor or work outside the home because of the dominant white culture's views on confining women to the domestic sphere. As feminist critic Paula Gunn Allen notes, these dramatic changes have resulted in a memory loss or cultural amnesia that has left many Native Americans disassociated from their cultures and vulnerable to systematic oppressions. Consequently, reminding their male counterparts of the significant role that their female ancestors played in countering colonization and resisting genocidal practices has become a key approach to reducing the oppression of Native American people as a whole.

Like other women of color in nationalist movements, Native American female activists struggled to be viewed as equal participants in the American Indian Movement. It was especially difficult to gain the mainstream media's attention. For instance, the 1973 siege at

Anna Mae Pictou-Aquash

In 1973, Anna Mae Pictou-Aquash was at the height of her activism. After earlier stints volunteering with the Boston Indian Council, where she helped newly arrived Native Americans acclimate to the big-city environment, and participating in protests at Plymouth Rock and in Washington, DC, where she marched in the Trail of Broken Treaties, Anna Mae was ready for a greater challenge. Learning of the Pine Ridge reservation takeover at Wounded Knee by the American Indian Movement (AIM), she quit her factory job, left her two daughters with a sister, and headed to South Dakota. Three years later, however, she was dead. Her murdered body was found at the bottom of a cliff on the edge of the Pine Ridge reservation, where it had lain exposed for two months. Anna Mae was only thirty years old.

Anna Mae Pictou was born March 27, 1945, on the Shubenacadie reservation in Nova Scotia. She belonged to the Mi'kmaq tribe and, like most of its members, grew up extremely poor. She had ambition, though, and at the age of seventeen decided to move to Boston with a boyfriend. Once there she began working for General Motors, married, gave birth to two children, and settled into a relatively comfortable life. However, once the political activism of the late 1960s began to take root, she quickly found herself ready to take part.

Native American feminist scholar Devon Abbott Mihesuah refers to Anna Mae as "a martyr for Native women and men who are freedom fighters, a symbol of both the courage of Native women and the possible fate of outspoken individuals who displease their government and members of their own organization." Much of what is known about Anna Mae certainly seems to fit this description. Anna Mae was one of the only women within the AIM organization to gain prominence. Her strength, intelligence, and dogged determinism made her a forceful figure despite being slight in size. Committed to her ideals and strategic in her pursuit of them, she was often considered "larger than life," as a *U.S. News and World Report* article suggests. Yet these same characteristics may have also led to her death. During the Pine Ridge takeover, Anna Mae managed to smuggle herself and her new boyfriend, Nogeeshik Aquash (divorced from her first husband, she later married Aquash while at Wounded Knee), past police barricades. Once inside the compound where AIM was holed up, she immediately took on an active role and, unlike the majority of the female AIM members, was able to use her previous karate training and strong physique to convince the men that she could participate in night patrol and do the physical labor of digging bunkers. These actions, argues Mihesuah, planted the seeds of suspicion against Anna Mae. She notes that most male AIM members preferred that their women remain in the background performing traditional, domestic duties. Anna Mae's free spirit made them uncomfortable. In addition, Mihesuah asserts, Anna Mae had grown up aware of her background, unlike many AIM members who first embraced their culture as adults. She spoke her tribe's language, knew its history and customs, and was familiar with the strong, matrilineal role that women once held. These factors set her apart from most of the AIM membership.

After the Pine Ridge takeover ended in bloodshed, the FBI became determined to dismantle AIM, and interactions with it led the group into greater violence. After a shooting between its officers and AIM members, the FBI sought to use Anna Mae as a witness against the individuals involved. Anna Mae went underground but was repeatedly found and arrested. Because she was quickly released each time, AIM members began to suspect she was working as an informant. Rumors started to circulate, and soon even her Canadian background, another marker of difference, became a source of distrust.

Once her body was found, the debate over who killed her began. AIM members accused the FBI of the murder. The FBI argued that all signs seemed to point at AIM. However, neither group launched a serious investigation, in part because both were to blame. In the late 1990s, as a result of her family's insistence and a couple of sympathetic police officers who persisted in pursuing the case because they felt the need to vindicate Anna Mae's death, suspicion fell on three low-ranked AIM members as being responsible for kidnapping and shooting her. The FBI also admitted that it had tried to cast doubt on her so that it could create tensions within the group, causing it to implode. To date, one of the men has been convicted in the killing, another has been indicted, and the third is awaiting trial.

Despite her tragic death, Anna Mae's presence continues to be significant. In 1999, family members established the ANNA foundation in

continued

continued from previous page
Arizona to honor her dream of improving the lives of all Native Americans. In addition, the Indigenous Women's Network has named an annual award after her. The controversy that defined her life is also not entirely gone. As the New York Times reported in 2003, new tensions between the government and former AIM leadership arose as the validity of another member's case came into question. Fellow AIM leader Leonard Peltier, convicted of multiple life sentences for deaths resulting from another confrontation between AIM and law enforcement, has repeatedly been denied an appeal to his case. Both sides in the case—his lawyers and the lawyers for the state—now point to the Pictou-Aquash case as cause for, respectively, his innocence and his guilt. Her murder illustrates the violence that was present in the organization as well as the reasons for its instigation. Either way, Anna Mae's life remains a catalyst for change.

the Pine Ridge/Wounded Knee reservation was largely the result of prompting by the elder female members of AIM who argued that the site was symbolically significant because of the number of lives that had been previously lost there during the massacre of 1890. However, once AIM took over Wounded Knee, the women were redirected to washing clothes, preparing food, and generally remaining in the background while the men dealt with the media and political negotiations.

The siege ended in bloodshed and gave the U.S. government an excuse to arrest the majority of the AIM membership. Much of the attention during the ensuing trials also focused on the men, whom the media cast as stereotypical male warriors. Meanwhile, Ho Chunk Indian Lorelei DeCora Means and Lakota Indian Madonna Gilbert Thunderhawk, two of the main figures among the eighty-five women charged, received almost no coverage and little financial support for their cases. Ironically, they were not even present at their own trials because they were too preoccupied with their organizing efforts.

The decision by women of color to remain active in nationalist organizations despite the sexual harassment, violence, and secondary status that most were assigned reflects the intersectional nature of their oppressions as much as their investment in ending them. As critical race theorist and law professor Kimberlé Crenshaw, who is largely credited with first applying the word "intersectionality" to the lives of women of color, explains, the term helps "describe the location of women of color both within overlapping systems of subordination and at the margins of feminism and antiracism." Women of color are diversely affected by the ways in which race and gender intersect. This makes their challenges to confronting racism and misogyny more difficult. It also leaves adopting only one strategy (for example, feminism or nationalism) ineffective. However, as Crenshaw indicates, most women in the 1960s and '70s found it more feasible to address gender issues within their communities than to struggle with white, middle-class feminists against race and class issues.

Bridging Identities

In 1977, the National Women's Studies Association (NWSA) was formed and its preamble pressed for a pluralist feminism that would address diverse forms of oppression and bias within academia. Specifically, the organization emphasized a political platform built on interconnectedness through multiple struggles for freedom, instead of basing it on the membership's demographic makeup, which was initially almost entirely white. Following a relational model that consciously avoided the patriarchal structure of the nuclear family, NWSA, and the women's movement more generally, frequently employed the slogan SISTERHOOD IS POWERFUL to increase a sense of affinity across cultural lines. Nevertheless, two years later, at NWSA's first conference, 93 percent of the participants were white, a number that decreased by only 1 percent in 1980. Although NWSA conference organizers tried to remedy the situation by directly addressing it in the 1981 conference, where the theme was "Women Respond to Racism," the results remained mixed. More women of color did attend; however, overall participation decreased (i.e., fewer white women showed up). The conference title itself also proved problematic since it located women apart from the issue of racism and once again emphasized a separation between gender and race. Indeed, most critiques of this 1981 effort focus on NWSA's inability to account for the "endemic racism within the women's movement," as scholar Elisabeth Armstrong writes in *The Retreat from Organization: U.S. Feminism Reconceptualized*. The same year, however, also brought hope for unity from a different direction; 1981 saw the publication of *This Bridge Called My Back: Writings by Radical Women of Color*, a collection that would forefront the intersections between race, class, gender, and sexuality in ways that would invariably transform traditional paradigms within U.S. feminism.

Edited by Gloria Anzaldúa and Cherríe Moraga, *This Bridge* directly wove together the political issues NWSA sought to explore with the personal experiences and emotions of the women who lived them. The essays and poems reflected both the anger and pain that women of color felt in their daily lives. Specifically, the contributors described the visibility and invisibility that the mainstream culture imposed on them, argued for a feminism that originated from their cultural background and experiences, addressed the debilitating effects of racism in the women's movement, and examined the differences that divide women of color from each other. In turn, the female body served as a metaphor for the physical toll that these issues took on women of color as well as the material energy that these female contributors were willing to expend to develop healthier relationships with others. In the words of Toni Cade Bambara, who wrote the foreword, "This Bridge lays down the planks to cross over on to a new place."

Reaching a new place required addressing not only race, gender, and class biases, but also homophobia and heterosexism. Many of the contributors in *This Bridge* were lesbians of color. As such, they lacked support from women of color who held onto heterosexual privilege as a way of avoiding further alienation. At the same time, white lesbians often treated lesbians of color with suspicion if they voiced concern for the men in their communities. This created a precarious position for lesbians of color who, like their heterosexual sisters, frequently shared close bonds with their male counterparts who experienced similar racial discrimination and economic challenges. Their relationships through kinship, culture, and social struggle precluded them from focusing exclusively on the issue of gender. As Barbara Smith and Beverly Smith explain in an interview included in *This Bridge*, "We are concerned with issues that affect our whole race. . . . And it's not like we like [men's] sexism or even want to sleep with them."

Although daunting, given the many possibilities for conflict, the promise of building bridges across cultures, identities, and politics was a driving force in *This Bridge*. As Moraga wrote, "To come to see each other as sisters. This is not a given. I keep wanting to repeat over and over again, the pain and shock of difference, the joy of commonness, the exhilaration of meeting through incredible odds against it." In fact, Moraga's excitement cannot be overstated. The particular isolation that lesbians of color experience is

86,000 Copies Sold

Winner Of The 1986 BEFORE COLUMBUS FOUNDATION AMERICAN BOOK AWARD

THIS BRIDGE CALLED MY BACK

WRITINGS BY RADICAL WOMEN OF COLOR

EDITORS:
CHERRÍE MORAGA
GLORIA ANZALDÚA
FOREWORD:
TONI CADE BAMBARA

Reprinted by permission of Cherríe Moraga and the estate of Gloria Anzaldúa

First published in 1981, This Bridge Called My Back: Writings by Radical Women of Color *was a groundbreaking collection that highlighted the intersections between race, class, gender, and sexuality.*

visceral real. In *Borderlands/La Frontera*, a text that Anzaldúa later wrote on her own, she mused on the irony of the word "homophobia" as she described her greatest pain in coming out: "Fear of going home. And of not being taken in. We're afraid of being abandoned by mother, the culture, *la Raza*, for being unacceptable, faulty, damaged. Most of us unconsciously believe that if we reveal this unacceptable aspect of the self our mother/culture/race will totally reject us." Shifting from fear to anger, Audre Lorde's direct plea to her community is equally moving: "I don't want to be tolerated, nor misnamed. I want to be recognized. I am a black lesbian, and I am your sister."

The concept of family, real or imagined, that lesbians of color emphasize is implicit in the social goals championed by the various nationalist movements and in the political unity that NWSA envisioned, and it certainly serves as a theme for this introductory chapter. It returns us to the belief in a *gente*, a people of our own. Yet at the same time, it calls into question the issue of who those people are—or can be—to us, given the multiple identities that we as women of color embody and contradict. Coming together as a politicized community, emphasizing a shared identity, or set of identities, despite differences can be particularly tough when we realize how many ideas of what is normal and desirable we ingest every day. Consider, for instance, how gay and lesbian individuals struggle daily for acceptance within heterosexual culture, yet transgendered men and women still occupy a largely marginalized position within the queer community. Ask yourselves why, if American-born Latinos are still largely working class and subject to stereotype and mistreatment by mainstream society, they are willing to ostracize and support xenophobic views of Latino immigrants. Similarly, why is it that Mizrahi Jews, many of whom have been displaced from various parts of the world but who are not Ashkenazi and of Eastern European heritage, are regularly omitted from discussions within the U.S. Jewish community about religious persecution? How do we account for difference within our communities?

The last day I was taking care of my niece, I decided to return to the local park. Once again, I found myself sharing space in the playground area, this time with a young Latina woman and her daughter. We took turns swinging the girls on the one swing that had a safety latch. After a while, we started talking. She confided that she was a single mother who lived with her family and was enrolled in community college. She told me she often thought her friends did not understand her situation. I found myself admitting how much it bothered me that people had assumed Annika and I were not related. As we spoke, I thought about the substantial differences between us. She had to find time to bring her daughter to the park. It was likely that this was their main outing, and a precious one at that, given her hectic schedule. Meanwhile, I was able to watch my niece while my sister vacationed in a faraway location because I can spend the summers away from the classroom. As a professor, I stood at the opposite end of her trajectory as a community college student. Yet here we were sharing our frustrations over the same concept of family, each of us offering the other one encouragement.

This seems to be one of the more positive consequences of intersectionality. Despite the different implications in our intersecting dynamics of race, class, and gender, the young mother and I created a kind of temporary intimacy and support as women of color. Indeed, the moment we shared reminds me of the end of Cherríe Moraga's play, *Giving Up the Ghost*, in which the young lesbian protagonist, Marissa, closes the scene on a surprisingly optimistic note, despite having experienced a number of crushing events. She tells the audience, "It's like making *familia* from scratch / each time all over again . . . with strangers / if I must. / If I must, I will." That day at the park, we both stayed a little longer than we anticipated, each finding comfort in our conversation and feeling, even if it was just briefly, like *familia*.

CHAPTER 2

EMBODIED REPRESENTATIONS

TOOT TOOT HEY BEEP BEEP. In 1979, disco diva Donna Summer (né LaDonna Gaines) had two smash hits that carried the same theme. Sung with a seductive brazenness by the African American Summer, "Bad Girls," an ode to "dirty bad" prostitutes who combed the streets at night, and "Hot Stuff," a sexually aggressive call out to find a "warm-blooded lover," both described wild women on the loose. In fact, the allure of Summer's sexy lyrics so captivated listeners that her initial breakout single, "Love to Love You Baby," which featured Summer's own (faked) orgasmic moans and groans, was quickly remixed into a seventeen-minute-long track that played in discos everywhere. Many argue that Summer helped usher in a new era for female music performers by making iconic the image of the disco queen with her songs about sexually liberated women set to pulsating background beats. However, Summer's rise to fame followed a familiar path for black women and recalled a much longer sexual history for many women of color in the United States and abroad.

Living in Europe during the early years of her career, Summer met songwriter-producers Giorgio Moroder and Pete Bellotte, who cowrote a number of songs for Summer that in 1974 resulted in her first full-length album, *Lady of the Night.* As its title suggests, the album created a sexual persona for Summer that set the stage for the trademark hit "Love to Love You Baby" and caught the attention of U.S.-based Casablanca Records. Its president, Neil Bogart, and Moroder soon began capitalizing on Summer's sexually charged image by producing a series of records that featured the singer cooing about various sexual exploits or coyly lamenting her fate as a lonely forsaken lover. Performed in revealing outfits that were meant to mirror the dance scene where her music played, Summer's live appearances further blurred the distinction between her and the wanton women she sang about. As critic Judy Kutulas contends, this called into question the reasoning for Summer's popularity.

In her essay "'You Probably Think This Song Is About You': 1970s Women's Music from Carole King to the Disco Divas," Kutulas sees "the looming presence of Moroder as a kind of producer-pimp [that] consigned [Summer] to the category of musical slut. Summer was a commodity, an object." Kutulas further argues that Summer's 1970s eroticized image consciously eschewed the proud Afrocentric iconography of the Black Power Movement in favor of whiteness and "stereotypes of African Americans as more sexual and passionate." Ultimately, Kutulas reads Summer as a sellout. More precisely, she posits her sexuality as the currency of exchange.

It is significant that Kutulas considers the adoption of the image of the black nationalist female rebel preferable to the hypersexual images of black women that have long circulated in mainstream popular culture. On the surface, the former certainly appears much more powerful and dignified, but memoirs such as those written by former Black Panthers Elaine Brown and Assata Shakur, who describe having to give up sex on demand and being physically abused by their male comrades, complicate an easy condemnation of Summer's decision (if she had one). Be it as a down-with-it soul sista or a reigning disco diva, neither role was completely freeing for Donna Summer or most black women of her era. Too many racist and patriarchal interpretations of their sexuality stood in the way.

Legacies of the Past

Historically, black women have struggled to control representations of their sexuality, and the line between their sexual agency and the sexual exploitation they face has often been blurred. While patriarchy subjects almost all women to some form of a virgin-whore sexual dichotomy (more commonly known as "good girls vs. bad"), women of color carry the extra burden of being judged through the additional prisms of race and class. The experiences of colonization create images of women of color that are based on racial identity and further affected by their class standing. In the case of African Americans, slavery set in motion a dynamic around black women's bodies that limits positive representations of their sexuality and their ability to play with sexual roles. As slaves, black women had to contend with the mandate that their bodies were someone else's property. That made their abuse— through forced impregnation, rape, and other forms of assault— justifiable and expected.

As a result, the complexity of African American women's sexual agency has been largely reduced to polar images of good and bad. Most conspicuous are the mammy and jezebel stereotypes, which surfaced during slavery and continued in its aftermath. Female slaves were largely relegated to fieldwork, but in wealthier homes many also provided domestic care. According to historian Patricia A. Turner, most house servants were young (few slaves lived long lives), relatively thin (food was scarce), and often mixed race and light skinned (a result of sexual intercourse between white owners and slaves). However, they rarely have been portrayed this way. The mammy caricature depicts house servants as elderly women with pitch-black skin and obese bodies. Emphasizing an overly maternal nature and joyful disposition, it also suggests a deep-seated loyalty and love for her owner's family and contentment with her situation. In contrast, the jezebel appears as a physically attractive mulatto who assumes power through sexual cunning. Considered promiscuous, the jezebel supposedly entices white men with her insatiable sexual appetite. The reality, however, is that mammies and jezebels were more frequently distortions of the same person.

Most female slaves were sexually exploited and objectified, indiscriminately. The distinction between "good" and "bad" black women was created to justify the different sexual roles that they were

© Corbis

The caricature of the mammy, which presented domestic slaves as loyal, nonthreatening, and content in their servitude, allowed viewers to see slavery as a benign institution.

forced to perform. As mammies, the emphasis was on their domestic duties. Making them appear old, dark, and obese served to desexualize them so as to diminish the threat of their presence in their owners' homes. The implication was that the owner and other male family members, who were already predisposed to see dark skin and overweight bodies as ugly, would not be attracted to a mammy and, thus, she would not disrupt the wife's place within the home. As a nursemaid to the children, the mammy had a cheerful attitude that eclipsed the fact that she was denied her own children, including often having to give her breast milk to the owner's children instead of her own. This docile image allowed white owners to appreciate the benefits of the black female body without feeling remorse over how those benefits were gotten. However, sexual relations between white men and female slaves did occur and rebellions did take place. Consequently, the figure of a scheming, self-serving jezebel offered an explanation when female slaves misbehaved.

The idea that people of African descent were innately lustful preceded U.S. slavery. European colonists in Africa regularly criticized the inhabitants' sexuality, often focusing on their lack of clothing as proof of their lasciviousness. Tying this flawed logic to other erroneous assumptions about intelligence, morality, and sophistication, Europeans justified their enslaving practices as necessary to their overall efforts to "civilize" the African continent. This polarization between cultures created a sharp contrast between Europeans and Africans. However,

Hottentot Venus

Born in 1789, during a period of great strife and violence in South Africa, Saartjie (pronounced "Saar-key") Baartman stands as one of the country's most emblematic figures of European colonialism. Known as the "Hottentot Venus," Saartjie was exhibited extensively throughout England and France as a female monstrosity. Specifically, Saartjie's buttocks and genitalia provided Europeans with "proof" that Africans were racially inferior, sexually primitive, and prone to perversion. In reality, however, Saartjie Baartman's tragic fate illustrates the far-reaching effects of racism and misogyny on the black female body.

"Hottentot" is a Dutch term that was derogatively applied to the Khoi Khoi people. Saartjie was a member of the Khoi Khoi clan, a prosperous cattle-herding tribe that populated much of the Cape Colony region in South Africa. However, after the arrival of Europeans at the start of the 18th century, life began to change as the colonists' interest in the country's land and resources led to battles with the country's governing tribes. By the time of Saartjie's birth, the Khoi Khoi had seen all of their wealth lost and the majority of their people killed or enslaved.

Saartjie was a direct victim of her community's upheaval. Her mother died shortly after her birth, and her father was killed during a land dispute when Saartjie was a teenager. Soon after, Saartjie was captured and taken to Capetown, where she was sold into servitude. She became the property of a freed black hunter who sent her to work as a maid and nanny for his brother's family. While in their service, Saartjie met Alexander Dunlop, a British military doctor who visited the home. Fascinated by her appearance, Dunlop became convinced that Europeans would pay great sums of money to view Saartjie's "unusual" physique. As scholar Sander L. Gilman explains, "The nineteenth century perceived the black female as possessing not only a 'primitive' sexual appetite, but also the external signs of this temperament, 'primitive' genitalia." As was traditional in her culture, Saartjie's labia and surrounding genitalia had been extended to form what Europeans called an "apron." While the practice was considered beautiful by Saartjie's tribe, and intended as part of a woman's initiation into

continued

continued from previous page

adulthood and marriage, as Gilman notes, Europeans took the alteration of her genitalia as a confirmation of the Africans' pathological nature. To Dunlop, this was part of the attraction. Naming Saartjie after the seductive goddess, Venus, he believed she would enthrall many viewers with her otherwise "repelling" features.

In 1810, Saartjie arrived with Dunlop in London at the age of twenty-two and almost immediately became a sensation. Scantily dressed with tribal ornaments, she stood on a stage while crowds paid handsomely to see her protruding buttocks. Because of obscenity laws, her apron was displayed only during private exhibitions. Abolitionists in London attempted to block Saartjie's performances and fought for her release. However, a court ruling determined that Saartjie had willingly entered into a contract with Dunlop and was not being mistreated. Because Saartjie was illiterate and may not have been clear about Dunlop's intentions, critics have long seen this decision as fraught with prejudice.

Eventually, the allure of an exotic, seminaked African woman faded in England, and Dunlop, quick to cut his losses, sold Saartjie to a French travelling circus. As part of the circus, she was displayed in a cage, billed as a freak, and even beaten on occasion. By 1815, the circus was losing money and decided to release Saartjie, penniless, into the street. She spent the next year getting by through prostitution. She suffered from alcoholism, and her health deteriorated. In 1816, Saartjie collapsed in her bathtub and died. While the cause of her death is unknown, many critics

the dialectic failed to account for their regular and close interactions that exposed more similarities than differences and disproved most of the colonists' biased views. In the case of U.S. slavery, the jezebel figure became a way to mediate between how a white society conceived of female slaves and who they actually were.

Most African women entered U.S. slavery through slave auctions, where they were often exhibited naked and exposed to humiliating physical examinations. From the outset, their sexuality was considered an object of public spectacle. This continued with a heavy focus placed on their sexual reproduction. Female slaves were frequently pregnant either as a result of force or coercion (work-free days or extra food believe that it was a combined result of her alcoholism and fatal pneumonia. Some also suggest that she may have had syphilis, which affected her nervous system. In either case, her death once again catapulted her into the limelight as doctors interested in promoting scientific arguments about race rushed to examine her body. Subsequently, her body was dissected and a plaster cast of it was made. Saartjie's brain, skeleton, genitalia, and body cast were then bought by the Musée de l'Homme in Paris, where her body parts were frequently exhibited until the mid-1980s.

With the fall of apartheid in the 1990s, interest in Saartjie once again resurfaced as demands for the return of her remains to South Africa grew more persistent. In fact, throughout the decades, many South Africans had waged campaigns for her return, each urging for a proper burial in her homeland. In 1994, then-president Nelson Mandela began to seriously negotiate the issue with French president François Mitterrand. At first, the Musée de l'Homme and other French museums protested, fearing this request would initiate others by countries that had been similarly "plundered by colonial adventurers." However, the significance of South Africa's political changes and the added pressure of women's rights activists, artists, academics, politicians, and international groups forced the French government to seriously consider the proposal. The bill passed, and on April 29, 2002, Saartjie Baartman's remains were turned over by the museum and sent to Johannesburg. One hundred eighty-seven years after Saartjie's departure, she was returned to her homeland and finally laid to rest.

were common incentives); even prepubescent girls were encouraged to become sexually active in order to prepare them to "breed." In a few rare cases, female slaves were also hired out as prostitutes. Each of these factors contributed to the notion that black women were hypersexual and obscured their actual position as victims of rape and exploitation. In turn, this gave white men—owners, male family members of owners, and field overseers—the excuse to dismiss any sexual misconduct on their part. They could recast their abuse as the result of falling prey to the female slave's wiles.

By focusing on female slaves' sexuality, the jezebel stereotype also redirected attention away from the significant ways that black female slaves deceived their owners. As activist and scholar Angela Davis asserts, slave women were far from docile. In "Reflections on the Black Woman's Roles in the Community of Slaves," Davis cites numerous examples of resistance that black female slaves waged against their owners to assist their own communities. Besides working toward buying relatives' and friends' freedom, slave women poisoned food and set fire to their masters' homes. They also participated in large-scale revolts, wielding weapons and risking death alongside their male counterparts. Even in minor ways such as feigning illness to avoid work, black female slaves countered their oppression. Yet despite such valiant efforts, it is the persistently negative images of black women as mammies and jezebels, frequently captured in popular culture (think of films such as *Gone with the Wind* and "Black Americana" collectibles), that remain vivid in the U.S. popular imagination. Similarly, it is the violence of these historical events that has left black women stigmatized and vulnerable to other negative representations.

During the Reconstruction period (1865–1877) immediately following slavery, the battle for sexual autonomy continued as many former female slaves moved north and became employed as domestic workers. As historian Darlene Clark Hine explains, the lack of other job opportunities and the low wages that drove most domestic work made it nearly impossible for black women to be economically self-sufficient. As a result, many relied on housing from their employers, an arrangement that increased the likelihood of their exploitation. In addition to facing unfair job demands and extended work schedules, black domestic workers found themselves subject to sexual advances by their employers. Even those who lived away from their place of employment faced challenges in exercising control over their bodies. Some found it financially necessary to engage in prostitution and other sex work, while others encountered sexual violence from men in their own families and communities. Yet despite the numerous affronts, few were willing to publicly acknowledge their situations.

Many black women chose instead to foster what Hine calls a "culture of dissemblance" around their shared experiences of sexual violence. To handle the trauma of sexual violence that could resurface at any moment, many black women learned to "dissemble," or conceal the truth of their inner lives. Hine suggests that their secrecy about rape or other forms of sexual assault that they experienced became a means of deflecting the already negative connotations attached to the black female body. The burden of sexual stigma rooted in the antebellum period, coupled with the shame and intimidation attached to their lives as "free" black women, made any mention of sexuality a precarious topic for discussion. Within their own community, it reopened wounds and threatened to expose how black men had internalized sexism and misogyny. To an outside, still largely prejudiced, white community, it confirmed claims of a degenerate morality. Indeed, until the late 20th century, any woman—regardless of race—who accused a man of sexual assault was immediately regarded with suspicion. For African American women, the racial dimensions of such a charge only intensified the issue.

Black women's marginalization within mainstream white culture made addressing physical safety singularly a black women's issue. As Hine notes, while the lynching of black men became a topic of public outcry and garnered wide attention, the rape of black women remained a minor point of commentary. More frequently, it was cited as another example of how black men were psychologically affected by failing to protect their women. Consequently, these factors shaped the focus that the issue of black female sexuality ultimately took. For black women, sexual autonomy became framed as a crusade for preserving their chastity, causing it to become even more deeply entrenched in discussions around class.

Black women were among the earliest advocates for legal protection against rape. In particular, women's clubs such as the National Association of Colored Women (NACW), founded in 1896, and the National Council of Negro Women (NCNW), founded in 1935, lobbied for specific legislation that would "defend their name." At the core of their protests was a subtext that black women's physical safety was inextricably tied to persistent accusations of immorality and sexual perversity. Advocates believed that as long as there was no legal recourse to prevent the sexual harassment of black women, their character would remain in question, making actual incidents of sexual assault more easily dismissible and further perpetuating stereotypes that dehumanized them.

Assumptions about black women also formed a barrier for those attempting to gain social mobility. General prejudice kept most African Americans shut out of the higher-class echelons. Any hint of an active sexuality was read as a confirmation of black hypersexuality and fueled arguments that the black community was inherently savage and less socially evolved. As a result, early crusaders worked extensively to downplay sexuality altogether, which along with the shame that the "culture of dissemblance" hid, eventually drove most expressions of black female sexuality underground. This made sexuality more often a source of repression. For the majority of black women who were also working class, it became a taboo subject to avoid at all costs.

The Politics of Sexuality

As we look at the mass proliferation of sexual imagery in our culture today, the negative history of black female sexuality might no longer appear relevant. Images of black sexuality—female and male—are abundant in the 21st century and, at first sight, seem rather distant from the manipulated images of mammies and jezebels. For instance, since Donna Summer's hits of the 1970s and '80s, more recent popular music has given us "female power" songs such as "Independent Women" by Destiny's Child and "A Woman's Worth" by Alicia Keys as well as numerous sexually explicit rap stars such as Lil' Kim and Missy Elliott, who argue for sexual pleasure on their own terms. Within the world of sports, tennis champs and sisters Venus and Serena Williams have transported the powerful nature of their physiques from the court, where it makes them exceptional athletes, to the store racks, where it helps them sell sexy sportswear and clothing lines. To some, examples such as these would suggest that black women have taken control of their historically hypersexualized portrayals precisely by exploiting them.

Yet as sociologist Patricia Hill Collins asserts in *Black Sexual Politics: African Americans, Gender, and the New Racism,* "In the post–civil rights era, gender has emerged as a prominent feature of what some call a 'new' racism." How people see African Americans as men and women as well as their perceptions of African American masculinity and femininity still affect the types of "opportunities and discrimination African American women and men encounter in schools, jobs, government agencies, and other American social institutions." In many ways, argues Collins, African Americans have not escaped the binds of the double consciousness that W. E. B. DuBois described before the civil rights period. Black men and women must still live in a culture saturated with stereotypical images that presume to represent them. In fact, she contends, to fully understand the far-reaching effects of racism on the African American community, one must consider how dominant representations of African Americans (including the mammy and jezebel images) meaningfully affect how African American men and women treat *each other.*

In 1974, a group of black feminists who called themselves the Combahee River Collective issued "A Black Feminist Statement," one of the most significant documents to address the interlocking issues of class, gender, and sexuality within the African American community. Describing a number of personal experiences, the essay illustrates why addressing the sexual politics within their own community is crucial to the overall survival of African American people as a whole. In the statement, members of the collective write about the pressure they felt growing up to conform to the standards of white culture—to be "quiet" and "ladylike"—and they address their growing awareness of the "threat of physical and sexual abuse by men."

Only later, as part of the collective, however, did the women realize the extent to which issues of gender and sexuality divided their community. For several of the women, these divisions became most apparent when they decided to pursue an education. As they write, "We discussed the ways in which our early intellectual interests had been attacked by our peers, particularly Black males. We discovered that all of us, because we were 'smart' had also been considered 'ugly,' i.e., 'smart-ugly.' 'Smart-ugly' crystallized the way in which most of us had been forced to develop our intellects at great cost to our 'social' lives. The sanctions in the Black and white communities against Black women thinkers is comparatively much higher than for white women, particularly ones from the educated middle and upper classes." Critics such as Collins would argue that the "sanctions" that the collective cites are central to the sexual politics that African Americans have internalized from the dominant culture and that perpetuate the sexism and misogyny against black women.

The term "smart-ugly" is likely to conjure memories of that brainy awkward girl from your high school days. As we know, beauty and intelligence are supposed to be mutually exclusive, but as we also know, there are indeed women who embody both qualities. However, what distinguishes this general characterization of women as either/or from the collective's term "smart-ugly" is that most young white women, especially those from higher classes, tend to belong to communities that support their intelligence and offer successful role models who look like them (i.e., white and female). There are far fewer examples and opportunities for young women of color. Indeed, for women of color who come from struggling communities, the decision to seek out an education is likely to place them in an isolated position and simultaneously distance them from their former surroundings. Thus, being smart comes with heavy consequences. For instance, the Combahee River Collective's members paid for exercising their intelligence by being outright ostracized and rejected by their black male counterparts. Their "social lives"—whether that meant dating, family gatherings, or friendships—were affected when they chose to educate themselves. What made them "ugly" to the men in their community was not their looks; it was the threat that their education posed. It was their ability to insert themselves into the community in ways that did not require them to be subordinate or docile. Beyond drawing out differences in class, being educated laid bare the unfair gender treatment that women received from men and led them to question why they had ever endured it.

While education inspires self-empowerment and can provide members of a community with a weapon to fight outside oppression, it also exposes problems that lurk *within* an oppressed community. Too often, black women are criticized for being overly aggressive, demanding, or even selfish, hence "ugly," when they seek to improve their lives. The implication is that, by choosing to pursue a course that can remove them from their immediate surroundings and make transparent class differences that also encompass gender discrimination, black women reject the supporting role that they are expected to play for men. In turn, falling back on the sexist notion that intelligent women are unattractive, black men—and the community itself—fail to account for their own oppression and rely instead on intimidation and blame to suppress their sisters and bolster a dangerously false sense of power/pride in black masculinity.

The 1992 rape case involving Mike Tyson and Rhode Island beauty contestant and college student Desiree Washington offers a good example of this scapegoating. Although one can speculate about what actually happened, the African American community's reaction to the rape charge against Tyson was stalwartly one sided, as Gayle Pollard-Terry reports in a *Los Angeles Times* story. Several male community leaders came out vehemently in his support and urged others to do the same. At one rally sponsored by the 8.5 million–member National Baptist Convention, the organization's then-president Reverend T. J. Jemison reminded the crowd, "Our brother needs us." Nation of Islam leader and cosponsor of the event Louis Farrakhan was cruder in his remarks: "You bring a hawk into the chicken yard and wonder why the chicken got eaten up. You bring Mike to a beauty contest and all these fine foxes just parading in front of Mike. Mike's eyes begin to dance like a hungry man looking at a Wendy's beef burger or something. She said, 'No, Mike, no.' I mean how many times, sisters, have you said 'No' and you mean 'Yes'?"

Both Jemison and Farrakhan exact loyalty from their black sisters and the community as a whole by using a language of guilt and blame. Moreover, their words underscore the persisting vestiges of slavery by encouraging a culture of silence and denial around the issue of rape. Embedded in their statements is the implication that women are sacrificial. In Farrakhan's case, he suggests that they are also likely duplicitous, which recalls the sexually negative images of the jezebel. Neither man acknowledges that many black women have suffered by *not* speaking out. As sexual assault expert and journalist Lori S. Robinson notes, many black women are in fact reluctant to report sexual assault because they feel compelled to protect the men in their communities and families. They are also wary of an unjust penal system and recognize the potential damage to families in removing men from their households. However, as women, their dedication to their community is often overlooked or taken for granted. More often, their race is emphasized against their gender and sexuality, which are both disparaged or ignored. Comments such as Jemison's and Farrakhan's emphatically make clear the depth to which the dominant culture's assumptions about the black female body have affected the black community's treatment of it. In addition, they illustrate the pervasive nature of the violence that surrounds black women's lives.

Colonizing Bodies

Foregrounding the history of black women in this chapter on sexuality offers an opportunity to create a comparative framework for looking at the experiences of other women of color. It also provides a contrast for discerning how issues of class, gender, and sexuality are often specific to one's racial/ethnic background. For example, how do Asian American women, Native American women, or Latinas fare in their own communities in relation to the experiences of colonialism, physical violence, sexual stereotyping, and exploitive capitalism? What overarching issues shape the lives of women of color that allow us to discuss their sexualities collectively? Similarly, how do different sexualities and gender identities (e.g., lesbianism, bisexuality, transgenderism) create particular discussions or crossover experiences between and among ethnic groups? Are there shared methods of resistance and subversive expression? And how is Donna Summer still relevant to these conversations?

Native American scholar and antiviolence activist Andrea Smith posits, "If sexual violence is not simply a tool of patriarchy but also a tool of colonialism and racism, then entire communities of color are the victims of sexual violence." Smith's assertion illuminates the reasoning behind Patricia Hill Collins's call for a sexual politics analysis. The sexual violence done to the bodies of women of color provides a paradigm for understanding how the dominant culture treats its communities as well as how the communities treat themselves. Consider how Rayna Green arrives at what she calls the "Pocahontas perplex."

Green argues that even before Europeans had the physical image of the princess Pocahontas to employ as an icon, they had already created the symbol of the Native woman to represent the New World. Depicted as similar to a Greek goddess but imbued with images of a wild nature, "the bare-breasted, Amazonian Native American Queen" appeared as "the sole representation for the Americas" from 1575 to 1765. The image recalled a nurturing Mother Nature figure whose body, or unfamiliar landscape, also presented danger and peril. She was admired but untamable. However, her daughter, the princess, raised with exposure to European settlers and knowledge of their ways, provided the necessary bridge to overcome these fears. The princess's youth made the feasibility of assimilating Native Americans into Western culture more possible in the settlers' imaginations and, as such, she was portrayed as bearing a physical resemblance to Europeans. Her nobility also bestowed her with a sense of purity and civility considered uniquely Western. By creating a female image that was more like them than like other Native Americans, Europeans, and later American settlers, conjured an acceptable partner for themselves. The discovery of Pocahontas, the Powhatan Indian who befriended Virginia settlers and supposedly saved one of their own from death, only served to bring to life this otherwise improbable female figure. Even so, there was only one Pocahontas, and the details of her story have always been dubious at best.

In Disney's animated version, Pocahontas not only defies her father to rescue John Smith, but she also falls deeply in love with the colonist.

This limited-edition Barbie doll features singer-actress Cher in a replica of the Native American costume that designer Bob Mackie created to promote her 1973 song "Half-Breed." Although Cher's Native American roots are sketchy at best, her over-the-top public displays depicting her heritage in the stereotypical representation of an Indian princess have been a hit with fans.

In actuality, Pocahontas married a different Englishman, John Rolfe, and it appears unlikely that she ever had any romantic feelings for Smith. There is also some doubt about the rescue. However, the intertwined elements of love and sacrifice are not lost in most tales told about their encounter. The supposed Pocahontas-Smith romance symbolizes the desire that Europeans often felt for Indian women and the submission to that desire that they imagined the women would be willing to provide. Here was a woman, noble and innocent, who willingly sacrificed herself, and possibly her people, for a rogue white male hero. Like the black mammy, the Native princess supported the colonizer's actions. Her presumed participation in his plans made her a co-conspirator and her benign character made her physically appealing. However, as they did for the mammy and the jezebel, these traits also presented a problem.

Tied up in their relationships to both white and Indian men, flesh-and-bone Indian women complicated the princess iconography. The princess's sexuality was attractive to colonists only as long as it was not exercised. However, real Indian women had Indian male partners, mothered Indian children, and were lusted after by white men. Consequently, as Green notes, "The Pocahontas perplex emerged as a controlling metaphor in the American experience." The "princess" was an abstraction that suggested that Indian women encouraged the conquest of their land and people. In reality, however, the concrete experiences of Indian women and the sexual violence they experienced through colonization required a different figure: the "darker, negatively viewed sister, the Squaw."

Rather than a fantasy colluder, explains Green, the squaw was a distorted scapegoat meant to relieve white men of the guilt they felt for their sexual attraction to Native women and the violence they perpetuated in response to it. To mask the colonizers' violence against the indigenous people of America, they cast Indian women as inherently savage. Like Indian men, squaws were constructed as possessing failing morals, including drunkenness, thievery, and laziness. In addition, as a female figure supposedly opposite of the princess, the squaw was depicted as lascivious, poor, fat, and ugly. Sound familiar?

Body Counts

In February 2000, the U.S. Department of Justice released a report that stated, "Native Americans are twice as likely to be victims of violent crime than any other group. They have the highest suicide rates in the nation. They are twice as likely as any other ethnic group to be arrested for an alcohol-related offense, and four times more likely to spend time in jail." More alarming, the report revealed that Native American women experience a level of violent crime that is nearly 50 percent higher than that reported by black males. According to an Amnesty International 2005–2006 study, homicide is the third-leading cause of death among Native American women, and they are victimized 2.5 times more often than other ethnic groups. In addition, one in three Native American women will be raped at some point in their lives, a rate that is more than double that for non-Native women. In most cases, their attackers are non-Native. Equally disturbing, domestic violence is extremely high in reservation communities, with more than 75 percent of murders of Native American women committed by someone they knew. These startling figures reveal the multiple sites of violence that intersect Native American women's lives. Like African

Yellow Woman

"Stories will help you be strong," asserts writer Leslie Marmon Silko. Growing up on a Laguna Pueblo Indian reservation in New Mexico, Silko often struggled to make sense of her mixed-race heritage. Her appearance made her different, and she realized this held the potential for isolation. Her relationship with her elders, however, and the stories they told, taught Silko to view her differences positively. In particular, the tales of Kochininako, or Yellow Woman, presented a role model whose very strength and allure were based on what set her apart. Yellow Woman was often drawn away from her people and engaged in acts that required courage and will. At the same time, she was a figure whose uninhibited sexuality defied stereotype. In her work, Silko revives Yellow Woman's complex representation to present her as a significant counterimage to the negative portrayals of Native American women that are so often perpetuated in mainstream American culture.

There are many stories of Yellow Woman's adventures, but the most common one entails her saving her people. A drought threatening to starve Yellow Woman's community forces her to venture out far away from her village in search of water. Happening upon a fresh spring, she stops to fill her water jar. However, she is interrupted when out of the pool emerges a handsome man dressed in buffalo skins. Inexplicably drawn to him, Yellow Woman has no time to react when the man transforms himself back into his original shape as Buffalo Man and whisks her off on his back. Together, they ride across the plains, falling deeply in love. Yellow Woman tells Buffalo Man of her community's struggles, and he responds by sending back his people so they can provide their bodies as food for her starving village. Eventually, she returns and her people warmly embrace her. In some versions of this tale, Yellow Woman is married, but her love affair is never condemned. In others, she brings back twin boys who eventually become heroes to the community.

There are other stories about Yellow Woman's adventures, as Silko notes. For example, in one tale, Yellow Woman is out hunting rabbits to feed her family and must outwit a monster that chases her. In another that

Silko wrote for her collection *Storyteller*, Yellow Woman is a modern-day, spiritually lost Native American woman who finds herself caught up in a liaison with a mysterious Navajo man named Silva who steals cattle from white ranchers. He repeatedly calls her Yellow Woman but she initially rejects the name, convinced it is part of a history that has died with her grandfather, who told the stories of Yellow Woman. Eventually, however, her journey with Silva becomes one of rediscovery, and upon returning home, she decides to become the new storyteller, ensuring not only the memory of her grandfather, but also that of this legendary figure.

Throughout these stories, Yellow Woman serves as a resource to her people by being different from them and sometimes going against social convention. As scholar Paula Gunn Allen notes, "The stories do not necessarily imply that difference is punishable; on the contrary, it is often her very difference that makes her special adventures possible, and these adventures often have happy outcomes for Kochinnenako and her people." Similarly, explains Silko, "Sometimes an individual must act despite disapproval, or concern for appearances or what others may say." Kept alive by the Keres people who inhabit the Laguna and Acoma Pueblos in New Mexico through the retelling of her passion and conviction, Yellow Woman provides Silko and other contemporary Native American women with a way of imagining themselves separate from the virgin-whore dichotomy that Western society imposes. Instead, for many, she is a reminder of their culture's powerful feminist history.

In addition, Yellow Woman's sexuality offers a positive example for women. Her sexual freedom is celebrated and considered empowering. As Silko emphasizes, sexual repression was a result of Western colonization and not natural to the ways of her people. Yellow Woman "has courage to act in times of great peril, and her triumph is achieved by her sensuality, not through violence and destruction." This latter point is key to understanding the significance of women within the greater cosmology of the Keres people. Yellow Woman's stories "emphasize her centrality to harmony, balance and prosperity of the tribe," explains Allen. For the mortal Native American woman, it similarly implies an acceptance and appreciation for the various differences that make women valuable to the whole community. Yellow Woman is a life-affirming creator and, as her female descendants, so can other Native American women be.

American women, Native American women experience violence in profound ways that demonstrate the extent to which issues of sexuality converge with those of race and gender.

In fact, the Pocahontas perplex's self-loathing squaw actively haunts the lives of contemporary Native American women. Working as a rape crisis counselor, feminist scholar and activist Andrea Smith discovered that every Native American female survivor she ever treated at some point admitted to her, "I wish I was no longer Indian." For these women, being sexually assaulted was intricately tied to being both female *and* Native American. They saw their violation as a consequence of possessing either or both of these characteristics. Like Green, Smith contends that the true origin of this dual victimization lies in the history of colonialism that American Indians suffered at the hands of European settlers. Exploitation of Native American female sexuality, she argues, was used as a means of exterminating a population and usurping its property: "The project of colonial sexual violence establishes the ideology that Native bodies are inherently violable—and by extension, that Native lands are also inherently violable."

Tracing the ideology that leads to the sexual dehumanization of Native American women begins with understanding how Manifest Destiny shaped much of the Euro-American expansion across the Americas. As European settlements gave way to an American government and Euro-American culture, a sociopolitical doctrine began to take form that assumed the United States had the ordained right and responsibility to spread its culture and acquire territory. By the mid-1800s, this concept of white supremacy and domination became actively employed to remove people from their lands and force them to assimilate to a Euro-American society. As a result, physical bodies became a primary target. Foremost, American colonizers organized their efforts as attempts to improve communities that they saw as essentially flawed. As their European forebears had done with African people, white Americans used stereotypes of Native American sexuality as justification for their actions against them. As Smith explains, "In the colonial imagination, Native bodies are . . . immanently polluted with sexual sin." This thinking eventually set forth a culture of violence toward Native American communities that had a direct impact on Native American women. Racist and patriarchal in nature, the violence that Native Americans experienced also fostered misogyny and self-hate among the tribes themselves.

In *The Sacred Hoop*, Paula Gunn Allen identifies the negative characterization and abuse of Native American women as a "synchronistic" result of colonization: "Patriarchy requires that powerful women be discredited so that its own system will seem to be the only one that reasonable or intelligent people can subscribe to." Before European contact, many tribes functioned as matrilineal cultures and women held a variety of leadership roles. Consequently, Allen argues, colonizing Native American communities required in part undermining the position of Native American women. Forcing women to lose political power and social status not only accelerated the subjugation of Native people, but it also shifted blame and anger toward women. Through time, this manifested itself through the community's own neglect and abuse of its women. As Smith notes, whereas before European contact tribes dealt swiftly with the few incidents of gender violence that occurred, as centuries passed, most became lax in their punishments and some Native American community members even came to view sexual violence as "traditional."

In addition, discrepancies between tribal justice systems and U.S. federal law enforcement often hinder the legal prosecution of sexual violence offenders. For example, Smith cites the various problems that arise from the simple fact that rape falls under the Major Crimes Act. Because the act limits the ability of Native American tribes to prosecute serious offenses, most tribes rely on the federal court system to handle rape cases and few have established codes of their own to address them. However, rape cases in general are difficult to pursue, and the added obstacle of having them occur on Indian territories leaves most U.S. attorneys unwilling to prosecute them. Furthermore, even when tribal courts attempt to try a rape case, the Indian Civil Rights Act (ICRA) of 1968 limits them to issuing maximum one-year sentences.

Yet perhaps most frustrating and symbolic of the "inherently violable" ideology of Native American women that Smith identifies is the fact that "tribes do not have the right to prosecute non-Indians for crimes that occur on reservations." At the same time, reservations are usually located far from state and county law enforcement agencies and officers themselves are often reluctant to respond to rape cases since they are not compensated for their time from either the federal government or tribal communities. Even when state or county law enforcement does arrive at a crime scene, it does not have jurisdiction on reservation lands. As Smith concludes, "So, unless state law enforcement is cross-deputized with tribal law enforcement, *no one* can arrest non-Native perpetrators of crimes on Native land."

Fatherly Fallacies

The broad sexual license with which Native American women's bodies have been treated is particularly troubling when considered alongside the frequent representations of white men as protectors of women of color. For instance, Paula Gunn Allen cites the hypocrisy of the U.S. government's insisting that tribes such as the Iroquois and Cherokee institute "democracy" in their communities before granting them federal recognition and protection, yet forcing them to adopt a democratic process by which the only officials given political power are men elected primarily by nontraditional community members. This is illustrated in the signing of the 1835 Treaty of New Echota, which resulted in the tremendous loss of the Cherokee Nation's Southeast territory. As historian Theda Perdue notes, no woman was included in the process. This exclusion signaled a dramatic shift from the traditional Cherokee ways of the previous century, when women had held significant positions of leadership. The paternalism that Allen and Perdue describe has been a crucial tool of colonization as men of color have adopted patriarchal practices but have still been forced to assume an inferior role within the colonizer's overall power structure. Moreover, the persistent depiction of men of color as hypersexual savages from whom white men must protect their women (and, in a benevolent gesture, also women of color) further encourages paternalism by promoting the notion that white men are heroes and defenders of civilization. In return, white men receive entitlement to the ownership (and violation) of women of color.

Paternalism is one of the greater forces shaping the sexual politics between communities of color and the dominant culture. Perhaps this is in part what makes Donna Summer's pop singer persona particularly objectionable when subjected to race and gender analysis. For all its titillating lyrics, most of Summer's early music projects the image of a sexually adventurous woman who nevertheless needs male guidance or direction. Indeed, the same can be said of Summer herself, who despite her own ambition relied on the assistance of men such as Moroder and Bogart to "make it" in the entertainment industry. Songs such as "Last Dance," in which Summer wants a lover "Beside me, to guide me / To hold me, to scold me," emphasize the same fantasies that male colonizers have long held about women of color in general. Lyrics such as these perpetuate a specific sexual myth in which women of color are inherently naughty and thus must be redeemed by the honor of white men. Through time, this distorted, uneven pairing can appear normal. In Summer's case, the racial weight of her music's paternalistic influence is felt even in her own self-directed recordings. "Dim All the Lights," the first song actually written by Summer herself, asks a lover to "turn my brown body white." Besides being one of her most risqué lyrics, the racialized subtext of this sexual wish remains glaringly clear.

In *Interracial Intimacy: The Regulation of Race and Romance*, law professor Rachel F. Moran examines the strictures against interracial relationships in the United States and the impact of the 1967 *Loving v. Virginia* ruling, which struck down antimiscegenation laws, on popular attitudes toward interracial marriage. Analyzing legal cases and delving into social histories and cultural mores, Moran describes numerous ways in which the regulation of intimacies between people of different ethnic communities has helped define racial identity, reinforce racial inequality, and uphold moral notions of white supremacy. At the same time, Moran discovers that the degree to which interracial relationships are still regarded negatively or are more readily accepted varies largely depending on the historically racialized images of sexuality of different ethnic groups. For example, she notes the significant difference between the "marry-out" rates for black women and those for Asian American women, both of whom come from ethnic groups that have been heavily stigmatized by racial stereotypes. While factors such as achieving higher levels of education and employment as well as outnumbering marriageable black men in the population should encourage greater outmarriage rates for black women, they continue to experience a relatively low incidence of interracial marriage, especially in comparison to black men. Moran credits this discrepancy to many of the reasons mentioned earlier in this chapter. Perceived as either hypersexual or asexual because of past legacies of slavery or considered too independent and self-sufficient in contemporary times, black women are frequently "caught in a double bind."

In contrast, Asian Americans across various ethnic groups, including Chinese, Japanese, Vietnamese, and Korean, have had steady outmarriage rates during the forty years since *Loving*. Specifically, Moran found that Asian American women had a much higher marry-out rate than their male counterparts. Because this disparity is not due to an imbalance in gender ratios or socioeconomics (the numbers of marriageable men and women are relatively equal), and both genders share a similar class spectrum, Moran suggests that racialized images of Asian and Asian American sexuality may offer a more plausible answer. Like Native American and black women, Asian American women have been subject to a sexual paradox. In their case, it involves being imagined as either hyperfeminine and sensual or wildly exotic and dangerous. In their relationships with white men, these contradictory assumptions, coupled with an American paternalism that emphasizes the role of white men as protectors and diminishes the significance of Asian masculinity, may account for part of the mutual attraction.

In the foreword to *Dragon Ladies: Asian American Feminists Breathe Fire*, sociologist Karin Aguilar-San Juan underscores the significance that the West's colonial interactions with Asian countries have had in shaping how Asian Americans are subsequently viewed. Similarly, as historian Gary Y. Okihiro notes, these interactions stretch as far back as the 5th century BC with Grecian representations of Asia. In fact, Europeans began trading, traveling, and living within various Asian countries long before Asians ever arrived in the Americas. However, as many of these encounters gave way to imperialist actions, Europeans, and later Americans, also became embroiled in extensive histories of conflict with Asia, many of which have led to multiple military occupations and negative propaganda justifying Western domination. In the aftermath of this violence, Asian women have often surfaced as an assumed part of the cache that comes with Western victories. Considered "spoils of war," Asian women have been typically portrayed as innocent, docile, and eager to be saved by Western armed forces (for example, remember Vietnamese freedom fighter Co Bao's dying scene with Rambo in the film *First Blood,* in which the gift of her necklace becomes his justification for launching a killing spree?). Their fragility as women, often resulting in racist monikers such as "lotus blossom" and "china doll," is also frequently emphasized. In particular, Asian women have been cast opposite to Western women, who are alternatively represented as strong and aggressive. Yet rather than realistic depictions, these characterizations more accurately reflect a gendered extension of Orientalism.

Orientalism, as postcolonial scholar Edward Said defines it, is an understanding of the Orient (a vague geographical term assigned to nation-states east of Europe, which initially meant the Middle East and later included places such as Asia as Europeans ventured farther east) as a monolithic group of people, experiences, and customs that are fundamentally contrary to those of the West. In particular, whereas Western Europe projected itself as rational, orderly, and sexually prudent, Westerners imagined the Orient as primitive, savage, and lustful. Although Orientalism is based on a series of constructed images, it has had a very material impact on how the East is treated by the West. In particular, it has propped up the idea that Western nations are inherently superior. As Okihiro writes in *Margins and Mainstreams:*

Asians in American History and Culture, "Whether because of race or culture, of biology or behavior, of physical appearance or social construct, Asians appeared immutable, engendered, and inferior. These differences . . . helped to define the European identity as a negation of its Other."

Thus, Asian women, and subsequently Asian American women, have had to battle both the marginalizing effects of Orientalism and the widespread gender discrimination that exists throughout both Asia and the West. In the process, their sexuality has served as the mediating ground. For example, in instances where Western control of Asian countries has been secured, such as after the end of World War II or the Korean War, Asian women have been imagined as devoted companions to American GIs stationed in their homelands. In turn, images of soldiers being pampered by Asian women—whether they are geishas, bar girls, or shy villagers—have filtered back to the United States in the form of commercial media. Films depicting Asian women as vulnerable and sexually accessible have encouraged many American men to subconsciously interpret their own sexual desires as a chivalrous act of liberation. However, left out of most wide-screen lenses are the countless women who were violated by soldiers from both their own countries and the United States. Similarly, the reality of circumstances that likely forced some women to serve as concubines or prostitutes (for instance, extreme poverty, political upheaval, the destruction of their communities) is similarly avoided in Western representations of Asian female sexuality. Even the offspring produced by the forced sexual encounters between soldiers and Asian women are conveniently erased from the exoticized landscapes of the East. Instead, Americans are repeatedly fed pornographic scenes such as the one with the Da Nang hooker in *Full Metal Jacket* who assures her potential soldier customers, "Me so horny. Me love you long time."

While the lotus blossom figure inspires mostly lust, her implicit sexuality opens the door for the creation of her darker sister: the sinister dragon lady. According to journalist Sonia Shah, the American use of the term "dragon lady" takes historical root in various reports that

CÀN
CHÁ-BÁ-ĐVÈI

© Bruno Barbey / Magnum Photos

Asian women have typically been portrayed as devoted companions to American GIs, but these depictions leave out the poverty and destruction that have often forced women into prostitution. Shown here is a Saigon bar where U.S. troops could find prostitutes and heroin during the war in Vietnam, 1971.

the *New York Times* published in the late 19th century about China's last and longest-reigning female ruler, the Dowager Empress Tzu-Hsi. The reports called her "an awful old harridan" and "the wicked witch of the East, a reptilian dragon lady," and the pejorative term stuck as a way of characterizing Asian women as evil and degenerate. More specifically, it served as a means of naming the misogynist distrust and xenophobia that Americans felt in equal amounts with their attraction for Asian women.

Asian women's entry into the United States has often varied from that of their male counterparts. For example, whereas during the 19th century most Asian men came as laborers set on returning home once they gained the necessary financial means, Asian women came for different reasons (though many participated in the same backbreaking

Korean Camptown Women

Like several other Asian countries during World War II, Korea saw its women violated and forced into sexual slavery as a result of Japan's military occupation. Throughout the war, tens of thousands of Asian women from places such as China, Burma, and the Philippines were recruited, kidnapped, and coerced into providing sexual services to Japanese soldiers. In Korea, these "comfort women" have become integral to the country's history. In particular, the guilt surrounding their abuse has led to their veneration as victims of war, and the country has made many efforts to compensate them for their harrowing experiences. The decades following these events, however, proved less kind to a different set of Korean women who faced a similar situation when the U.S. military arrived in 1945 to occupy the country.

After World War II, U.S. troops were stationed in Korea as peacekeepers and offered protection against the rising communist threat in North Korea during the Korean War (1950–1953). However, their long-standing presence in the country had several negative and deteriorating effects. Initially, clearing the land to create the U.S. military bases resulted in the widespread displacement of rural village life. Businesses popped up that catered specifically to American soldiers. The areas surrounding the military bases soon became centers of criminal activity that included drugs, black markets, and a thriving sex trade. At the same time, devastated by consecutive wars, Korea soon found itself dependent on American dollars. For the next three decades, the country looked almost entirely to the U.S. military bases stationed around the country to support its economy. At one point, notes *JoongAng Daily* reporter Soo-Mee Park, "Camptown prostitution and related businesses on the Korean Peninsula contributed to nearly 25 percent of the Korean GNP."

Gijich'on, as Koreans called American "camptowns," or brothel districts, were central to the country's financial arrangement with the United States. As Park explains, camptowns were primarily set up to offer U.S. soldiers easy access to sexual services "in a controllable, confined area." Young women from displaced villages and those seeking reprieve from the country's crushing poverty were easily lured to work in the camptowns. Some went willingly, believing they would earn money to help themselves and their families. Others arrived with hopes of marrying American soldiers who could provide them with better, more comfortable lives. Still others, however, were deceived into becoming *"yangbuin,"* a term coined specifically to describe Korean bar girls and sex workers. They did not realize that working at an American camptown almost invariably entailed being a prostitute to U.S. soldiers. Once at the camptowns, women found it financially difficult to leave as most became indebted to the bar and club owners. In fact, none of these women had any financial means, most were uneducated, and many were alone in the world. Although much of the country still considers their decision to engage in prostitution a personal choice, others argue that their limited circumstances left camptown workers with few other options.

Another significant charge sympathizers wage in favor of camptown women is that Korea willingly supported the American brothels. As one former sex worker Park interviewed told him, "I remember how the government authorities hopped around from one club to another and taught us how to deal with G.I.s. They called us patriots and civil diplomats at the time, because we were helping to earn foreign currency and improve the U.S.-Korea alliance." Historian Ji-Yeon Yuh also notes the Korean government's active participation in funding brothels such as "American Town," which was built in 1969 by a South Korean general and landowner. Every day, buses filled with soldiers from military bases around the country filed in and out of the camptown, which operated approximately "twenty clubs, a dozen stores, and a government-run health clinic where the women receive[d] mandatory testing for sexually transmitted diseases." Eventually, American Town became so prosperous that the owners turned it into a corporation and sold shares to investors.

Despite the number of examples illustrating Korea's involvement in maintaining the camptowns, there is still a strong prejudice against the women who worked in them. Some critics argue that the former sex workers are an all-too-vivid reminder of the country's shameful past. Their experiences also detract from the image of sexual modesty still culturally imposed on Korean women. Unlike the World War II comfort women Yuh cites as "innocent victims of Japanese colonial aggression," camptown women are "dismissed" as anomalies who remain outsiders to Korean society. Yet many of the former camptown women, now in their sixties and seventies, refuse to be erased from the country's consciousness and have launched campaigns against the Korean government requesting housing and pension benefits. They argue that, like comfort women, they, too, are war victims.

work). Some women immigrated because they were joining fiancés or husbands. So-called "picture brides" married men they had never met. Other female immigrants came to escape poverty and the gender subjugation they experienced in countries where women faced even more restrictions than in the United States. For instance, several women chose immigration over having to remain widows or entering into arranged marriages against their will. Some hoped for the opportunity to gain a shot at education and greater personal freedom. Still others intentionally deserted abusive husbands.

Many fewer women than men made the journey to the United States. Between 1899 and 1924, Korean women made up only one-fifth of the approximately eight thousand Koreans who immigrated to Hawaii and the mainland. From 1920 to 1929, less than 1 percent of the nearly seventy-four thousand Filipino residents in Hawaii were women. According to the 1900 U.S. Census, only 410 of 24,326 Japanese were women. For the few Chinese women who arrived in the United States, primarily in San Francisco, besides being greatly outnumbered, the likelihood of sexual exploitation left them even further isolated. According to historian Judy Yung, in 1860 more than 80 percent of the Chinese female population in San Francisco was engaged in prostitution. The majority of these women were kidnapped or tricked by Chinese men who pimped them out to other men or exhibited them as freaks for their bound feet. In response, Americans, particularly white female missionaries, launched crusades against this treatment; however, their efforts often resulted in mistaking *all* Chinese women as prostitutes, casting an indiscriminate shadow of doubt over the virtue of any Asian woman (Chinese women alone were blamed for transmitting venereal disease and leading white men into lives of sin, despite the comparable number of white prostitutes). Their efforts also spread an overall prejudice against people of Asian descent as being morally depraved and out to corrupt the American way of life. It was also through the bodies of these victims of sexual exploitation that the caricature of the dragon lady breathed new life. As economic downturn and heightened xenophobia fueled anger toward Chinese male laborers,

Chinese women became the other half of an imagined evil pair. Fears of yellow peril encouraged Americans to see Chinese men as diabolical schemers set on dominating the world and Chinese women as their malicious, dragon lady accomplices.

Through time, repeated accusations of treachery and actualized cases of violence (for example, lynchings, beatings, and the infamous Japanese internment during World War II), and the general exclusion they experienced from mainstream American life, led many Asian Americans of different ethnic communities to avoid speaking out against their mistreatment. This is not to say that Asian Americans did not pursue social justice or were complacent in their marginalization. However, there was a degree of silencing, self-imposed and publicly sanctioned, that distinguished them from other ethnic groups in the United States and frequently caused them to be wrongly classified as a homogenous group of individuals who presumably had no reason to complain. As many white Americans erroneously assumed that their perseverance, strong work ethic, and the general determination to succeed were extensions of their supposedly quiet natures, rather than common characteristics among most immigrants, Asian Americans came to be viewed as "model minorities."

Beyond encouraging hostility with other ethnic groups, the model minority myth obscures the fact that Asian Americans experience many of the same struggles as other groups. Asian American women, as Mitsuye Yamada describes it, become dually "invisible" through their gender and race. The relative lack of attention to domestic violence among Asian Americans offers a good example. As the study *(Un)heard Voices: Domestic Violence in the Asian American Community* notes, "Asian American women have to deal with the constraints of their own cultures as well as those of an indifferent mainstream culture that denies that domestic violence occurs amongst Asian Americans. As a result, most battered Asian women gain very little assistance from systems that are supposed to help them find a measure of safety." Even when domestic violence is acknowledged, mainstream U.S. society can often misinterpret it as part of some cultural tradition that prevents Asians and Asian Americans from realizing that violence against women is wrong. This mentality was certainly present in the 1989 *New York v. Dong Lu Chen* court decision in which Chen's murder of his wife, Jian Wan, resulted in only a five-year probation. After learning that his wife had been having an affair, Chen assaulted her with a hammer, hitting her eight times and killing her. The judge hearing the case believed Chen's violence resulted from the Chinese culture's intolerance of female adultery. Chen's actions, in turn, were seen as a kind of defense of culture and family values. Ultimately, Asian American women such as Jian Wan not only lack protection within the U.S. legal system, but they are also denied justice after their victimization, leaving them dually invisible to the American eye.

"So Many Gay All Over the World"

In her stand-up concert *I'm the One That I Want*, Asian American and bisexual comedienne Margaret Cho describes her mother's response to the fact she might be gay. In broken English, Cho mimics her mother leaving a message on her answering machine asking Cho why she has not discussed the matter with her. "You have a cool mommy. Mommy is so cool and Mommy know all about the gay," Cho's mother assures her. "There are so many gay. So many gay, you know, all over, all over the world . . . so many gay, so many gay all over the world, but *not Korea, not Korea*!"

Funny as it is, Cho's joke could easily be refashioned for almost any ethnic community. Within many U.S. communities of color, sexualities other than heterosexuality are still largely viewed as external to the culture. Being queer, whether that means gay, lesbian, bisexual, or transgendered, is often assumed to be another uneasy by-product of American assimilation. While there are multiple roots of this denial, two interlocking reasons are the general lack of complex representations of people of color in mainstream society and the crushing force of compulsory heterosexuality. "Compulsory heterosexuality," a term coined by poet and essayist Adrienne Rich, addresses the belief that emotional and sexual bonds between men and women are primary and inherent, thus encouraging the notion that heterosexuality is a universal norm. Rich challenged this assumption by using the term to emphasize how a heterosexual norm goes unexamined in our society, leaving those who do not conform to be punished for it. Arguing that the institutionalization of heterosexuality (e.g., through religion, legal practices, family customs, popular culture) is what drives people to form heterosexual relationships, she suggests that heterosexuality is more often a result of social conditioning. Consequently, queer individuals become erased from public consciousness. For queer communities of color, which are also marked by racial and often class difference and affected by internalized modes of misogyny and sexual violence, the erasure can seem absolute. Yet in fact, queer communities of color offer perhaps some of the best examples of resistance to the heterosexual norm.

In "Chicana Lesbians: Fear and Loathing in the Chicano Community," Carla Trujillo argues how the very nature of their sexuality places Chicana lesbians in a position contrary to the cultural expectations for women. While the dominant practice of Catholicism in the Chicana/o culture generally discourages women from attaining sexual knowledge and the culture's patriarchal structure keeps them locked in a subordinate position, Chicana lesbians rebuke both restrictions when they "bring [their] sexuality into consciousness." Lesbianism initiates a space to reclaim a positive female sexuality and allows Chicanas to become unfettered from the social devices used to enforce sexual submission, such as motherhood and religion.

While compulsory heterosexuality and the cultural focus on family teach Chicanas that they should seek a male partner in order to fulfill their maternal role, Chicana lesbians who become mothers do so without remaining tied to this formula. Consequently, they are able to reject the material and emotional trappings that can come with requiring men to be central to the family structure. Similarly, Chicana lesbians who practice Catholicism must confront the indoctrination of heterosexuality and female submission that the religion upholds. While their resolve can involve either making deliberate compromises

Josefa Loaiza

Josefa Loaiza was a young Mexican woman who lived in Downieville, California, a thriving mining town near Sacramento, during the Gold Rush (1848–1855) era. She is also the only known woman ever to have been hanged in the state of California. Josefa was hanged by a mob because she killed an Anglo man who she claimed assaulted her. Although little more is known about her, Josefa has become a significant figure in Gold Rush lore. Throughout newspapers, magazines, personal diaries, and scholarly texts, she is discussed in terms that frequently draw assumptions about her appearance, sexual behavior, ethnic background, and class. Specifically, many cast her innocence—or guilt—in light of what they imagine it meant to be a poor woman of color living in an area surrounded by gold-thirsty, lovelorn men.

Josefa's execution occurred during the first year of California's admission into the union. Late into the evening of Downieville's inaugural Fourth of July celebration, a miner named Fredrick Cannon and his friends were walking along the town's Main Street. The men were intoxicated and as they stumbled along, they came across the home where Josefa and her husband, José, lived. Cannon knocked their door off its leather hinges and entered. Josefa was there alone. A short while later, Cannon emerged and the men continued on their way. But Cannon returned the following day. He needed hangover medication, and his doctor lived near the couple. When Cannon passed their doorway, José came out and began insisting that Cannon pay for the broken door. Cannon refused, and the two argued in Spanish, with Josefa soon joining the debate. The argument grew more heated as Cannon began calling Josefa a whore. In the ensuing exchange, Josefa dared Cannon to repeat his insults to her inside her home. She then retreated and he followed. When Cannon entered, she stabbed him in the heart, and he stumbled out, dying soon after. José and Josefa were taken into custody and a tribunal was hastily set up. John Rose, a local rancher, dubbed "Judge Lynch" by reporters at the scene, presided over the case. During the trial, a few residents tried to intervene on Josefa's behalf, but an angry mob soon turned on them as well. A few hours later, Josefa was sentenced to death, and José was run out of town. Josefa accepted her fate and was escorted down a long pathway to a makeshift platform on a bridge, where she was hanged. Her last words as she placed the noose over her own head were said to be, "I would do the same again if I was so provoked."

The will that Josefa showed in her actions has often been cited as a reason for whether or not her killing was justified. In particular, while feelings of racial distrust and discrimination ran high because of greed over gold and land claims, they existed in tandem with the intense sexual frustration that men felt because of the scarcity of women in the area. As a poor Mexican woman, Josefa thus inhabited a precarious position. A subject of both attraction and repulsion, she broke several social codes when she murdered one of Downieville's own. Defendants of the town's decision to punish her actions with death have blamed Josefa, as a Mexican woman, for being inherently prone to violence. They have also questioned her character, implying that she was a sexually loose woman who largely provoked the problem because of her bad temperament. Yet others argue that Josefa was likely a victim of sexual assault. They see her actions as inverting the gender dynamic that existed between her and the dominant white male culture that surrounded and desired her. In not only killing her assailant but also publicly admitting that she rightfully defended her honor, Josefa Loaiza emerges as an active participant in redefining her role as a Mexican woman living in the often violent environment of the Gold Rush. In either case, her execution and its subsequent retellings reveal the gendered politics of race and class in early California. Josefa was neither entirely innocent nor a bloodthirsty killer; she was one of the many Mexican women who have been erased from American history.

or leaving the church altogether, they are forced into an act of self-awareness that stands as a model of liberation for all women.

Understanding the destabilizing force of sexually rebellious female figures within the Chicana/o community requires looking back to its Mexican roots. Recognized as a manifestation of the Virgin Mary by the Roman Catholic Church, the Mexican Virgen de Guadalupe nevertheless possesses her own iconography. She is often called the "brown virgin" as her visage is darker than the Virgin Mary's and the symbols that surround her recall a specifically indigenous background that mirrors her followers' cultural past. With her bowed head and clasped hands, she is considered a powerful image of hope to Mexicans and Chicana/os, who identify her with struggle. However, for women, she has long held a more complicated meaning. Her subordinate stance and permanent suffering encourage the notion that women are meant to accept pain. Similarly, the implausible nature of being both a mother and a virgin makes her a very difficult role model to emulate. Yet most Mexican and Chicana women grow up being told to follow her example. To avoid this expectation, argues writer Sandra Cisneros, Mexican and Chicana women must either reconfigure her image in their own likeness or else look to actual flesh-and-bone women who have been equally formidable. As she concludes, "My *Virgen de Guadalupe* is not the mother of God. She is God. She is a face for a god without a face, an *indígena* for a god without ethnicity, a female deity for a god who is genderless, but I also understand that for her to approach me, for me to finally open the door and accept her, she had to be a woman like me."

In contrast to La Virgen, the other woman who looms equally large in the Mexican/Chicana/o cultural imagination is La Malinche, a historical figure who served as translator and lover to the Spanish conquistador Hernán Cortés in 1519. Originally named Malinal, she was an Aztec woman who was sold into slavery by her mother after her father's death. Malinal ended up as part of the cache that Cortés and his army accumulated as they made their way through Mexico into the Aztec capital of Tenochtitlán (now known as Mexico City).

Although Malinal was one of many women acquired by Cortés's men, she soon distinguished herself through the multiple languages she spoke. Recognizing her usefulness in negotiating with the diverse native communities that populated the Aztec empire, Cortés took her as his own assistant. It is this turn of fate that has made La Malinche a figure of contempt to many Mexicans and a symbol of power to many feminists.

As a translator, Malinal soon gained prominence among both the Spaniards and the indigenous communities they dealt with. Through her translations, she sealed deals for Cortés, prevented his capture, and ultimately aided him in bringing down Montezuma, the last Aztec ruler. Her pivotal role earned her respect from both cultures. As evidence, scholar Cordelia Candelaria cites the different names she was called. The Spanish referred to her as Doña Marina. An honorific title, the surname "Doña" is surprising given the disparaging opinions that most Spanish held toward indigenous people. The fact that she was an indigenous *woman* makes the moniker even more telling. Similarly, Malinal's compatriots soon began calling her Malintzin. As Candelaria explains, the suffix "-tzin" is also an honorific title, indicating that her own people also held her in high regard. Again, given the traditionally patriarchal nature of the Aztec community, this renaming is significant. The name Malinche appears to have been a linguistic evolution of Malintzin, according to Candelaria. However, as critics such as the contemporary writer Octavio Paz found, it could also serve as a means of permanently condemning a woman who braved the violence and upheaval that faced her community by relying on her extraordinary abilities alone.

In 1950, Paz published *The Labyrinth of Solitude*, a collection of essays on Mexican history and culture. The book received international acclaim and established Paz as a key social commentator on his country's affairs. Among the collection was an essay titled "Sons of La Malinche." Like Candelaria, Paz also took up the meaning behind Malinche's name. However, to him, it signaled the reason for contemporary Mexico's own turmoil and angst. Extrapolating on the linguistic origin of La

Malinche's name, he argued that the Mexican cuss word *"Chingada"* found its root in this historical figure's name. Translated crudely as "fucked," *Chingada* with its feminine "a" ending and its passive verb tense referred specifically to a woman, Paz claimed, even though it was used toward both men and women. Unique to the Mexican culture and used solely to express anger and violence, *Chingada,* he asserted, recalled the passive Indian woman who had let Cortés "fuck" not only her, but her entire country. As her unwilling sons, he continued, Mexican men were eternally subjected to the same sort of psychological trauma.

While feminists have long criticized Paz's misogynist interpretation, partly because of his essay, the phrase "La Malinche" has nevertheless become synonymous with being a traitorous whore. During the 1970s Chicano Movement, women who challenged the men's sexism were often accused of being Malinches. In Mexico, the term *malinchismo* is still regularly applied to someone who exploits the country, such as the many corrupt politicians who have historically bankrupted it.

The moralistic opinion regarding female sexuality has similarly remained engrained in the culture's consciousness. The belief that there are good women and there are bad women has allowed victimizations such as the ones taking place along the U.S.–Mexico bordertown of Juárez to continue without serious reprimand. In more than a decade, the overall death toll of women abducted and killed in this area has ranged from four hundred to eight hundred, with several hundred more reported missing. There does not appear to be one source to the violence; rather, drug cartels, gangs, and individual men all seem responsible for inflicting these terrible murders, which often also include sexual violence. The typical profile given for these victims is that they are young, poor women who have moved to the area alone to work in the maquiladora plants. These factors have been used as a pretense by Mexican law enforcement to suggest that these women are somehow responsible for what has happened to them because they are breaking away from traditional roles. However, other women with families, female students, middle-class women, and sex workers have also been killed. Such victimization of women of color, and the subsequent blaming of them for their own victimization, relies on hundreds of years of patriarchal and colonial domination and the virgin/whore images that arise out of these histories.

The question over choice in representation is a difficult one for women of color. How women of color are viewed is heavily mediated through the stereotypes and assumptions that have historically preceded them. The desire to divide women into acceptable and nonredeemable categories to justify their mistreatment only serves to destroy communities. In addition, the implications of the sexual histories experienced as a result of colonialism, racism, and patriarchy must necessarily be taken into account. Sandra Cisneros suggests that women look to others like themselves for self-reflection. This is what perhaps makes the example of singer Donna Summer most interesting at the close of this discussion. What does her image tell us about other women like her? What does she ultimately represent? Moreover, can she or any other woman of color ever escape sexual stereotyping as long as these questions remain unaddressed?

CHAPTER 3

SOCIAL STRUGGLES

JACQUELYN WAS A STUDENT in a women's studies class I taught on community service. The objective of the course was to give students the opportunity to put their feminist knowledge into practice by volunteering at various community organizations that provided assistance to women. Jacquelyn chose one of the tougher centers. Throughout the semester, she worked with a program that helped female military veterans get their lives back on track. The women in the program had all been homeless, most were survivors of sexual trauma, and many also suffered from drug and alcohol addiction. Jacquelyn was asked to create workshops to educate them on various topics. She decided to run her first one on body image and female sexuality. The response was not positive. From the outset, the workshop participants were resistant. They snickered when they saw the young, pretty woman stand up and introduce herself. As soon as she started her presentation, the women started their comments. *Who does she think she is? Shit, I have children older than her. She ain't got nothing to tell me I don't already know. This is bullshit.* Jacquelyn did not get very far in her presentation that day, but she persevered.

For the next ten weeks, Jacquelyn continued to visit the center. Sometimes she assisted her class peers with their presentations. Other times she helped with the office work. She never presented her own workshop again, but she did keep talking to the women. In class,

Jacquelyn shared some of her frustrations. She admitted feeling intimidated, and she questioned her ability to translate her feminist classroom experience to real-life activism. In this respect, she was not alone. Most of her classmates, all self-declared feminists, also found it difficult to apply feminism in a practical sense. Those tutoring younger girls at an after-school center did not feel comfortable using the "f" word. They thought it might scare the girls off. A group that was working with a local politician felt censored by the city government rhetoric that dictated their plans to create a local event honoring World War II female aircraft workers. The students who were advocates for domestic violence survivors had difficulty accepting when their clients failed to leave their abusers or to show up for court hearings.

I offered different pieces of advice to each of them, but I generally saw their struggles as a good thing. The world that exists outside the feminist classroom is not ideal, and feminism alone cannot shape change. Similarly, although women may be at the center of the issues, the activism that takes place does not always fall under the category of feminism. Several of the students, including Jacquelyn, were women of color, as were most of the girls and women they were working with. To put their feminist training into practice, the students had to learn to use it in ways that tapped into related sources of activism, such as antipoverty work or antiracism. They had to handle their differences with those they were serving in a collective manner. They also needed to understand the multiple layers of identity that shaped the lives of the women they were attempting to help. Spreading feminism, as most hoped to do, and encouraging others to assume a feminist identity was tied to addressing the material problems that these women faced, such as dealing with addictions, lacking stable home environments, or surviving teen peer pressures, in ways that might never actually engage the theoretical language of feminism.

In several ways, the students' struggles recalled the push and pull that women of color have historically experienced with white feminists over various social issues. Whereas their white sisters might have perceived a problem strictly in gender and sexuality terms, women of color found themselves responding to the racial and class factors that were also present. Although never separate, these factors sometimes came first for women of color. In discussing racism within the 1970s women's liberation movement, activist and scholar Angela Davis clarifies the misconception that women of color were either unaware of the sexism they faced or too preoccupied with nationalist struggles. She posits instead that white activists working on issues such as abortion overlooked *how* women of color negotiated their gender against other factors in their lives, such as race and class. This chapter thus takes its cue from Davis by examining three significant areas facing women of color—health, incarceration, and reproductive rights—and the numerous interrelated struggles that they encompass. In particular, these three areas illustrate how the bodies of women of color have been subject to abuse and control specifically as a result of racism and poverty. They also reveal intersecting strategies of resistance that jointly address race, class, gender, and sexuality. These strategies attempt to reverse the historical effects of colonialism and negative representation that are often responsible for perpetuating the physical mistreatment of women of color.

Health: Healing Against the Odds

While most agree that preventive care is key to avoiding future costly illnesses, various social and cultural factors can keep women of color from receiving even the most elementary healthcare services. For example, gaining access to medical help can feel impossible for those unfamiliar with the healthcare system or its language. In other cases, previous negative experiences can leave women hesitant to seek assistance for anything other than major health problems. Economics can also limit access. Those who lack insurance or who are underinsured are often reluctant to shoulder yet another financial burden. Even women who do regularly see a physician can miss out on preventive care since office visits do not always include prescreenings. As numerous studies indicate, few doctors routinely provide patients with dietary counseling or check for hypertension and diabetes. Failing to receive these examinations can take a heavy toll on women of color, who often come from communities that have historically battled illnesses related to these health risks.

Identifying health problems in women of color can be doubly difficult because they may coincide with other problems. Take, for example, writer Siobhan Brooks's recollection of her mother's isolating battle with schizophrenia. "For a Black woman to be depressed was seen as a type of luxury," recalls Brooks in "Black Feminism in Everyday Life: Race, Mental Illness, Poverty and Motherhood." Out of need, the people at the Sunnydale Housing Projects in San Francisco, where Brooks was raised, often accepted their poverty and the stresses that came with it as a normal part of their daily lives. As she explains, "The Black women I grew up with prided themselves on being 'strong Black women' . . . [they] prided themselves on raising children, supporting men and their families on low wages—without health care, let alone mental health care." In the case of Brooks's mother, despite erratic behavior and bouts in mental hospitals, she was able to pay their bills, maintain a household, and resist public assistance. This made her functional in her neighbors' eyes and thus minimized the actual severity of her condition. Nevertheless, while such a show of willpower has ensured the survival of many a community, it can also foster an individual belief in self-sacrifice.

As clinical psychologist Carla K. Bradshaw notes in "Asian and Asian American Women: Historical and Political Considerations in Psychotherapy," Asian American communities can also be reluctant to use mental health resources. Although the reasons are complex and often vary depending on factors such as gender, place of birth, and education, studies indicate that professional mental health treatments are underused among most Asian Americans. In part, there is still a certain amount of social stigma attached to admitting to emotional distress, and many individuals initially attempt to cope on their own before turning to professional help. As a result, preventive care is often neglected and those suffering from mental illness receive assistance only after their conditions have grown critical. The tragic experience of renowned author Iris Chang offers a case in point.

At age twenty-nine, Chang exposed one of the most provocative and previously untold wartime stories in history. In *The Rape of Nanking: The Forgotten Holocaust of World War II*, Chang detailed Japan's 1937 occupation of China's capital city, which lasted a week and resulted in widespread massacre. Praise and criticism for the book drew Chang into the public spotlight and she soon began advocating for an official apology from Japan and reparations for Nanking survivors. At the same time, however, Chang began showing signs of bipolar disorder. According to the *San Francisco Chronicle,* where her life was profiled, Chang dismissed her early symptoms as a result of lacking sufficient will. Instead, she threw herself into a series of new projects, including producing another book. She also gave birth to a son. Ultimately, this exacerbated Chang's mental deterioration. She soon grew anxious and collapsed from exhaustion. This led to a short period of therapy and on-again, off-again medication, with her family and friends also offering their support. In the end, however, Chang decided to end her pain by committing suicide on November 8, 2004. She was thirty-six.

Chang's experience is not isolated. According to the Department of Health and Human Services, Asian American women ages fifteen to twenty-four have the highest suicide rate of women of any race or ethnic group in that age category. Suicide is the second-leading cause of death among young Asian American women. Because Chang was a well-known and much admired figure in the Asian American community, her death set off an alarm for many. Performance artist Kristina Wong, in particular, used it as a catalyst to directly confront the issue. In *Wong Flew Over the Cuckoo's Nest,* Wong satirizes the treatment of mental illness in the Asian American community and addresses the general obstacles to seeking help. Using humor, she focuses on the various pressures that Asian American women frequently face that can instigate anxiety. Wong also illustrates the impossible standards to which Asian American women sometimes hold themselves by having her protagonist claim that she will solve her community's problems with depression and suicide within the show's ninety-minute span. In several instances, the show's portrayals of different mental health issues have proved so

© Antonia Kao/Divine Eye Productions

Kristina Wong confronted issues of mental illness in Asian American communities in her solo performance piece Wong Flew Over the Cuckoo's Nest.

moving that audience members later approached Wong about their own traumatic experiences. As a result, she often enlists mental health professionals to provide services at her performances. In doing so, Wong tangibly demonstrates the value of accepting therapeutic aid.

Like mental health, substance abuse and addiction problems are also areas in which women of color can encounter inadequate and irrelevant treatment with limited sensitivity or awareness of specific gender, racial, and cultural issues. For example, being unable to understand English or feeling as if they cannot clearly communicate their needs can frustrate women and dissuade them from seeking treatment. Employing a translator to discuss taboo subjects such as drug abuse is also not helpful; it can result in conveying inaccurate information because women are more likely to downplay their experiences. Similarly, traditional treatment programs can sometimes overlook the central source of support that the family offers in communities of color. Children are a primary reason women seek treatment, but fear about the safety and care of their children while they are in treatment is also a main factor in poor retention rates in inpatient treatment programs. In addition, this issue extends to post-treatment recovery since affordable childcare and parenting education continue to be needs for women attempting to reconstruct their lives.

Women of color are also susceptible to initiating alcohol and drug use at younger ages than the general population. For instance, a study by the Substance Abuse and Mental Health Services Administration (SAMHSA) found that Native American girls under age seventeen have a particularly high rate of substance use. The reasons for the use are varied but include socioeconomic factors such as low educational achievement, high unemployment, and, according to some researchers, a genetically predisposed susceptibility to alcoholism. Similarly, according to the 2001 National Household Survey on Drug Abuse, also published by SAMHSA, a significant number of young Latinas are turning to alcohol and illicit drugs. Almost one in five Latinas ages twelve to seventeen reported past-year illicit drug use. More than one in four reported lifetime use of an illicit drug. Almost one-third, 31 percent, reported past-year alcohol use. Often, their contact with drugs and alcohol is tied to their intimate relationships. For example, many Latinas admit to trying a substance as a way of being "supportive" of partners who use drugs or alcohol.

The use of alcohol and illicit drugs can also affect the degree to which women of color have safe sex. As the reproductive rights and sexual health organization Advocates for Youth reports, heterosexual contact is the most common reason women of color become infected with HIV. This includes having sex with a man who uses injection drugs, is HIV infected, or whose HIV status is unknown to his female partner. Latinas and African American women are particularly at risk. In 2001, HIV/AIDS was the leading cause of death for African American women ages twenty-five to thirty-four and the fifth-leading cause of death for Latinas in the same age category. The American Psychological Association also cautions that while HIV/AIDS diagnoses for Asian American and Native American women comprise only 1 percent of all diagnoses combined, lack of detailed HIV/AIDS data, underreporting of HIV/AIDS cases, and racial/ethnic misclassification could mask the true impact of HIV/AIDS within these communities.

Cultural differences also contribute to the rising figures regarding HIV and sexually transmitted infections (STIs) among women of color. For example, trusting a male partner who is not monogamous is a serious risk factor for any woman. However, the risk is further exacerbated in communities where addressing topics such as condom use, disease, and sexual behaviors is uncommon or taboo. In addition, the cultural imperative that women be submissive (for example, in Latino and Asian communities) can directly conflict with prevention strategies that ask women to be assertive, to negotiate safer sex, and to be responsible for their own sexual health. Communication can also be a barrier for Native Americans. While terms such as "HIV" and "AIDS" do not translate easily or clearly in many Native American languages, geographic location and differing customs also make prevention outreach difficult.

In addition, Native American and African American communities have a history of being abused in unethical U.S. government–sponsored experiments. For example, the 1932 Tuskegee syphilis study of black men allowed 399 patients to go untreated while scientists tracked the progression of their disease. The study was supposed to run for six months but instead lasted forty years. The men were never informed of the study's intent and received only free medical exams, free meals, and burial insurance in exchange for their participation. Similarly, in 1982, pharmaceutical companies targeted Alaska Native children for a hepatitis B trial vaccine program. Children who visited public health facilities in the Yukon Delta region were administered the experimental Heptavax B vaccine without parental consent. The rationale health professionals gave was that Alaska Natives were at high risk for the disease. However, as activist and scholar Andrea Smith argues, this claim contradicts other studies that indicate that Alaska Natives are no more at risk than any other group. Furthermore, she links the Heptavax B vaccination campaign to several other coercive efforts to use indigenous communities for trial drug programs. Abuses such as these have left a legacy of mistrust and misinformation regarding public health messages among communities of color. Many have simply convinced themselves that what they hear is not true.

Yet activists such as Stella Luna and Paulette Hogan refuse to remain silent about the issues of life and death facing their communities. Both women contracted HIV through heterosexual relationships. As Luna writes in "HIV and Me: The Chicana Version," she discovered she was HIV positive when she was given a routine blood test during the first month of her pregnancy. A man whom she had dated briefly before marrying her second husband infected her. Upon receiving her diagnosis, Luna was advised to terminate her pregnancy. She and her husband decided against it. The baby was born healthy but also HIV positive. As Luna began to control their conditions with medications, she grew eager for outside support. Her husband, in contrast, withdrew. Luna joined a group of women who varied from IV drug users to college students and housewives—all "women who didn't understand how this had ever happened to them." In time, this interaction became the impetus for her transformation into an advocate for services to HIV/AIDS-infected women and children. She helped establish a city task force, became a public speaker, and enrolled in college, where she majored in Chicana/o studies. Although it indirectly caused her divorce, Luna's HIV diagnosis became the center of her politicization. It became her way of advocating for better health options and encouraging a more open dialogue in her community about sexuality.

For Hogan, being HIV positive led her to push African American churches in a new direction. Profiled in a *Los Angeles Times* feature story, Hogan contracted HIV from a relationship she had after her divorce. She thought it was monogamous. Until then, Hogan had been an active member in her community, had several friends, and sang in her church choir. After the news of her diagnosis, Hogan's community began to shun her. Neighbors no longer wanted her children to play with theirs. Friends disappeared, rumors spread, and for two years, Hogan retreated to her home and her children. Through time, however, Hogan changed her outlook. She decided to date again, she started speaking to local community and high school groups, and she returned to the church. Her reentry was not subtle. As reporter Daniel Costello notes, she chose one of her church's more popular services and sat in the front row. Her bravado led one of the ministers to ask her to sing for the congregation. When Hogan took the microphone for the first time, she announced to the fifteen hundred–person crowd that she was "a woman living with HIV. And I am glad to be home."

Since then, Hogan has assisted her church in organizing a World AIDS Day event and honoring other AIDS activists. She has also had a direct influence in changing the role of African American churches in addressing the HIV/AIDS crisis in their communities. Although churches can serve as a central distributor of information and assistance, many pastors' negative attitudes toward homosexuality and IV drug use make it difficult to discuss HIV infection. The church's denial and silence have led many to avoid getting tested or to keep quiet about their illnesses. Hogan's visible presence in her church and community helps challenge this silence. Her face brings a familiarity to HIV that is difficult to ignore.

Organizing communities around health issues also requires looking at the external agents involved. As concerns about the environment gain visibility, problems that have disproportionately plagued poor people of color also surface. Activist groups in the environmental justice movement have been fighting such diverse problems as toxic/hazardous waste dumping, biosphere destruction, and chronic illnesses related to labor conditions (for example, asbestos, pesticides, lead poisoning) for several decades now. Indeed, for Native Americans, whose ecologically conscious practices extend back centuries, the struggle is even longer. However, recent mainstream interest in these issues and the growing outcomes of globalization are forcing discussions about environmental racism to take center stage. The environmental justice movement examines why communities of color are targeted more often for the dumping of pollutants and the construction of hazardous waste and maintenance sites. It also pushes for studies about how urban planning correlates with issues of race and class. For example, replacing green space with commercial space results in fewer opportunities for residents who lack yards to exercise or participate in leisure activities. Similarly, communities where "cancer clusters" have developed are often found adjacent to dense industrial activity.

In 1994, President Bill Clinton signed Executive Order 12898, Environmental Justice for Low Income and Minority Populations. The order directed federal agencies to develop strategies for identifying and removing environmental hazards that disproportionately affect minority and low-income populations. The order's signing was considered a victory by environmental activists and was expected to significantly reduce racial disparities. However, as Daniel Faber argues in *Capitalizing on Environmental Injustice*, things have only worsened. Back in 1980, the Reagan administration passed an initial environmental policy that was dubbed the "Superfund." Superfund allowed federal authorities to clean up large areas where hazardous materials threatened to harm nearby residents. Businesses found to be associated with the dumping of these materials were also held responsible for contributing to the cleanup costs. However, enactment of the policy was almost impossible from the start because of insufficient federal funding. Similarly, successful lobbying by big companies minimized penalties and financial responsibility. Clinton's order, almost fifteen years later, should have finally remedied these problems. Instead, Faber finds that the Superfund list of designated cleanup sites now contains seven times fewer low-income and minority population areas than it did back in the 1990s. In other words, if a hazardous site is discovered on Native American land, it will likely never make the Superfund list. Meanwhile, corporations continue to pour in money to block efforts to hold them accountable.

Yet while government efforts stall, grassroots organizers continue to forge ahead. In New York alone, advocate and scholar Julie Sze found several examples of environmental justice activism. Neighborhood organizing against water pollution, garbage privatization, and energy deregulation as well as families' efforts to combat the rising rates of children's asthma have transformed many ordinary citizens into agents of social change. As Sze emphasizes in *Noxious New York: The Racial Politics of Urban Health and Environmental Justice*, improving the environment does not have to be an "us versus them" struggle. A recentered focus on "the lives of those usually disenfranchised from the policy process: the young and the old, the working class and people of color" can create "better policy and environmental conditions for everyone."

Mothers of East Los Angeles

Ask a public relations specialist to describe what an environmental activist looks like, and she or he will likely tell you that the activist comes from a middle- or upper-class background, possesses a high level of education, and is fairly young. Meet one of the members of the grassroots group Mothers of East Los Angeles, and you'll discover just the opposite. At least that was what the California state government realized when it hired a public relations firm in 1986 to determine the best place to avoid opposition to a waste incinerator that it intended to erect. Aiming for locations where residents were poor, older, and significantly less educated appeared to be the best bet. In fact, this strategy seemed especially effective when you consider that, as sociologist Mary Pardo asserts, in 1990, three out of five African Americans and Latinos in California lived near toxic waste sites, "and three of the five largest hazardous waste landfills operated in communities with at least 80 percent minority populations." Nevertheless, statistics such as these did not deter a group of older women in their forties and fifties living in the Boyle Heights and East Los Angeles communities from organizing against both the incinerator slotted for the neighboring city of Vernon and a proposed plan to construct a state prison within the Boyle Heights area.

Headed by then–California governor George Deukmejian, the two projects were expected to face little resistance given the communities' assumed "political apathy." However, the projects' proponents underestimated the strong ties between local political representatives, the Catholic Church, and the long-standing Mexican American community that both of these groups served. At the time, many of the core activists who came to be involved in Mothers of East Los Angeles (MELA) were already engaged in securing safe and educational environments for their children through school parents' clubs and Neighborhood Watch associations. All of them were active members in their local churches. In addition, having lived in the area for more than thirty years, most had witnessed changes to their communities that left them wary of city planning. In the 1950s, for example, residents had been displaced multiple times to make room for new freeways. Each time, people received only brief notice and had no voice in the actual building process. Still, other female members who became involved in MELA had led fairly traditional lives until that point. As Pardo notes, "The process of activism also transformed previously 'invisible' women, making them not only visible but the center of public attention."

When word of building a prison in Boyle Heights first got out, local representatives from then-Assemblywoman Gloria Molina's office began contacting businesses and organizations in the area. They wanted to determine the community's response. This led to several concerned businessmen protesting the issue and flying to Sacramento to lobby against the prison proposal. However, after noticing the lack of female participants, Molina, a well-known feminist advocate, began requesting that more women get involved. Monsignor John Moretta of the Resurrection Catholic Parish became the solution to that problem. After hearing of the need for more female representation, he called a meeting with all of his female parishioners and laid out the problems with the prison proposal. He urged the women to get involved, and then he went one step further. Inspired by the activism of a group of Argentine women known as Las Madres de Plaza Mayo, who had rallied against a dangerous military dictatorship in order to have their "disappeared" children returned, Moretta suggested naming the group the Mothers of East Los Angeles. The women agreed, and not only was an organization born, but also a new way to reimagine the purpose and meaning of being a Latina mother.

As Pardo explains, "MELA transformed the definition of 'mother' to include militant political opposition to state-proposed projects they see as adverse to the quality of life in the community." MELA member Erlinda Robles underscored the communal sense of mothering: "When you are fighting for a better life for children and 'doing' for them, isn't that what mothers do? So we're all mothers. You don't have to have children to be a 'mother.'" The group was also not women-only. For example, its chief financial officer, Aurora Castillo, pointed out that not only did husbands support their wives, drive them to meetings, and participate in the discussions, they also made placards, worked security, and marched alongside the women during protests.

In the end, both the incinerator and prison state projects were abandoned. The success MELA experienced led to partnerships with various other environmental and social justice groups. In recent years, MELA helped stop a proposed oil pipeline project, which would have run partially through East Los Angeles and exposed the community to hazardous leaking while conveniently bypassing affluent communities altogether. In 1992, California Assemblywoman Lucille Roybal-Allard presented a resolution to MELA for its outstanding work. While issues surrounding environmental racism remain pervasive, MELA's strong foundational support and seamless intersection between family and community offer an unexpected face to the struggle.

Prison: Bending Back the Bars

On August 28, 1974, only three years after the infamous Attica rebellion at the upstate New York men's prison that left at least thirty-nine dead and brought international attention to the rampant human rights abuse in the U.S. prison system, a group of female inmates at another state prison staged a similar standoff. Protesting the beating of a fellow inmate, the prisoners at Bedford Hills Correctional Facility for Women, the largest maximum-security facility in New York, held seven employees hostage in a two-and-one-half–hour siege. The following year, a group of female inmates on the other side of the nation at a California prison also rebelled. Responding to the unexpected cancellation of family Christmas visits and packages, the women assembled in the prison yard, where they smashed windows and fueled a bonfire with the yard's Christmas tree displays. Neither event ever garnered much public recognition during its time. Only recently, in Victoria Law's *Resistance Behind Bars: The Struggles of Incarcerated Women,* has their significance come to bear as part of the burgeoning activism for female prisoners' rights.

Law argues that these two rebellions along with several others failed to gain publicity because women led them. Although according to 2005 U.S. Department of Justice figures women make up 7 percent of the overall U.S. prison population, the frequently deplorable conditions and neglect that female inmates experience continue to be overlooked. Nevertheless, female inmates have sustained a long history of organizing. Moreover, because women of color represent more than 47 percent of the female incarcerated community, many are also leading figures in generating this activism.

According to penal abolitionist and black feminist Julia Sudbury, the rate at which women are incarcerated in the United States has greatly increased during the last two decades. At the same time, as criminologist Cyndi Banks notes, more than half of those women imprisoned are African American or Latina. These numbers are striking given that each group of women still comprises less than 20 percent of the total U.S. population of women. Native Americans (including Alaskan Natives) fare no better. In many states, they account for two to three times more of the inmate population than their ethnic group's representation in the state population. The experiences of incarceration for women also vary significantly from those of their male counterparts. In addition to their organizing efforts being largely ignored, the gender-specific needs of female inmates rarely receive serious consideration. In areas such as healthcare, physical safety, and motherhood, female prisoners embody the intersecting oppressions of racism, sexism, classism, and homophobia in their daily struggles to survive the experience of being locked up.

Banks attributes part of the sharp rise in U.S. incarceration to stiffer penalties for drug abuse. Heavily promoted during the 1980s by the Reagan administration, the "War on Drugs" prohibition campaign led to more severe sentencing for even minor offenses. State-run programs were similarly harsh as lawmakers realized the opportunity to increase their popularity by passing tough-on-crime bills. For instance, in 1994, then–California governor Pete Wilson helped usher in the "three-strikes" law, which mandated a sentence of twenty-five years to life imprisonment for anyone convicted of any felony if that person had been previously convicted of two or more serious or violent felonies. While the law was initially met with overwhelming public support, since its passage, many have tried to have it revoked. As the Washington, DC–based organization Justice Policy Institute found in a 2004 study, the costly bill has had little impact on decreasing violent crimes. Furthermore, different interpretations of its application have sometimes led to discriminatory treatment and misuse of the law. For example, one former Los Angeles district attorney sought a life sentence for an ex-convict accused of stealing a slice of pizza. In addition, the Justice Policy Institute's report revealed that blacks were imprisoned under the three-strikes law at ten times the rate of whites, while the rate for Hispanics was almost 80 percent greater than for whites. In all cases, those most affected by these tougher laws are poor individuals who cannot afford to pay heavy fines or hire private legal representation to avoid jail time. Again, because women of color are

PEDRO VERDUZCO
29 YEARS TO LIFE
FOR
.6 GRAMS OF
DRUG POSSESSION

© AP Photo / Damian Dovarganes

Women of color have been at the forefront of the movement against California's "three strikes" law. Here, a girl whose father was sentenced under the law attends a protest organized by Families to Amend California's Three Strikes (FACTS) and other groups.

among the poorest populations in the United States, they are found more often behind bars.

Socioeconomic factors also contribute to the increase in female incarceration. Most female inmates are poorly educated and tend to have more than the average number of children. Many female inmates are also battling drug and alcohol addictions or mental illnesses. In addition, some female inmates have histories of physical and sexual abuse, which can lead them to duplicate this violence by becoming involved in abusive relationships. In some cases, these relationships have ended in women striking back and murdering their abusers. Some women also have gone to prison for drug charges or theft (sometimes for items under $150) because they were accomplices to criminal acts that their male partners committed.

To foster a path of independence and self-reliance, activists are focusing on education as a central tool for change. For example, at the Bedford Hills prison, women are finding ways to escape vicious social cycles by taking advantage of an educational partnership between Marymount Manhattan College and the prison. In 1997, the college stepped in when federal and state programs to educate prisoners stopped. Aimed at reducing recidivism, the college program offers prisoners an opportunity to earn an associate degree. For example, as a 2002 U.S. Department of Justice study revealed, the recidivism rate in 1994 for female inmates was as high as 58 percent. Yet for several participants interviewed in a promotional video for the Bedford

Hills-Marymount Manhattan program, the education they received goes beyond leaving prison for good; it allowed them to reinvent themselves. Many describe it as owning something "priceless." One inmate proudly stated, "I just know that that's something that the department of corrections or no one can take from me because it's here [pointing to her head]." Several women also believe they could be role models for younger women at risk. As one inmate puts it, "Each one, teach one."

While obtaining healthcare has become increasingly challenging for most average Americans, few realize the extent to which female prisoners are denied even the most essential medical resources and treatments. For example, pregnancy and chronic and degenerative diseases are particularly neglected. As Amnesty International reports, seriously ill inmates frequently fail to receive any kind of medical assistance. Consequently, even those with easily managed illnesses such as asthma and diabetes can develop life-threatening conditions that lead to death or permanent injury. The experience of Gina Muniz, who was serving a life sentence at a California state prison resulting from a $200 theft, offers a particularly harrowing example. The Seattle-based Women Behind Bars Project describes how Muniz's crime and first-time arrest was "bizarrely classified" as a carjacking although no one was harmed and no car was stolen. Muniz had stolen the money to feed a drug addiction she developed after her father's death. Believing she was pleading guilty to a seven-year conviction based on her lawyer's advice, she received life imprisonment instead. During her stay in the county jail and before being transferred to state prison, Muniz was diagnosed with cervical cancer. Because it was detected early, Muniz's condition was treatable. However, the disease went unattended, and six months later she was dead.

Drug use and prostitution are common, often interrelated charges among female inmates. In particular, the ongoing criminalization of sex work leaves women who engage in sexual acts for money without recourse. For example, when they are assaulted or cheated by a client and try to seek assistance from the police, they are usually threatened with arrest. This isolation places them at a higher risk for contracting or transmitting HIV. In general, the HIV infection rate is substantially higher in the prison population than in the general one, and when compared to male prisoners, women test positively more often. As the *Washington Post* reported in 2007, a study conducted in one DC jail facility found that women were infected at a rate nearly triple that of male prisoners. While knowing this fact would seem to make HIV treatment more successful among inmates, screening is not a federal requirement and many prisoners are released before treatment can be established.

Prisons also have limited medical facilities. Even personal hygiene can pose a challenge. For instance, given limited supplies, women are often forced to share or reuse sanitary napkins. Since specialized healthcare for women is usually situated off-site, addressing gynecological concerns such as sexually transmitted diseases, reproductive health problems, and high-risk pregnancies is even more prohibitive. In addition, prisons are often reluctant to transport inmates because of cost and limited time. Women who are treated are almost uniformly kept shackled during their examinations. For pregnant women, this includes during labor.

One bright spot in this ongoing problem is the activist push to allow female prisoners to keep their babies after giving birth. Rather than immediately taking the children away and placing them with relatives or in foster care, some innovative prison programs are allowing mothers to keep their newborns with them for a time. Eight states now offer these alternative programs. For example, in South Dakota babies are allowed to stay thirty days, and in Washington one facility allows mothers up to three years with their children. Programs such as these are especially important given that 52 percent of state inmates and 63 percent of federal inmates are parents. Sustained contact with their incarcerated parents lowers the chance that children will eventually follow the same destructive patterns and increases the likelihood that parents will remain out of prison once released.

Even when female prisoners are physically healthy, their safety can be compromised by custodial sexual misconduct. The majority of guards at most female prisons are still men. In reported cases of abuse, correctional officials were accused of subjecting female inmates to rape, other sexual assault, sexual extortion, and groping during body searches. Guards also watched women undress, shower, and use the toilet. When inmates complained, they often faced numerous forms of retaliation. However, this did not stop more than five hundred Michigan female prisoners from filing a class-action lawsuit in 1996 against the Michigan Department of Corrections. For fifteen years, the state of Michigan ignored complaints from female inmates about abuse at its facilities. Even when the U.S. Department of Justice ruled that the inmates' constitutional rights were being violated, the state did nothing. Yet despite the consistent disregard, several women pursued their cases and eventually persuaded a lawyer to intervene. To date, eighteen women have been awarded $50 million in damages and more trials are under way.

The record growth of prisons has led many to realize the industry's moneymaking potential. The prison industrial complex (PIC), as it is called, refers to the various organizations and businesses that profit from human incarceration. These include such diverse entities as prison guard unions, construction companies, surveillance technology vendors, governments and corporations seeking cheap/free labor pools, and Wall Street investors. Rather than encouraging rehabilitation, these groups have a vested interest in seeing incarceration rates go up.

Despite these obstacles, some facilities are attempting to work against state-supported violence. One women's prison in Vermont offers an especially inspiring example. The Dale Correctional Facility houses only 45 inmates. Its small size has allowed better use of programming and staff resources. The Vermont Women's Prison Project, which videotaped in-depth interviews with twenty-five incarcerated women, captured some of the ways that imprisonment could improve the inmates' lives. Despite "the inherent frustrations, difficulties, pain and suffering they all experienced from being locked up," prisoners at Dale used their time there to change their lives and find new direction. Through counseling, building support networks with each other, gaining job skills, learning about parenting, and fostering a positive all-

INCITE! Women Against Violence

Consider for a moment the image that comes to mind when you hear the phrase "violence against women." More than likely, it is the same one that most people picture: a woman battered by a man who is usually a boyfriend or husband. Fewer people, however, are apt to take into account the sociopolitical forces that can also cause violence against women. For instance, how often do you think of police officers or prison guards in relation to assaults against women? How about the military or the medical industry? When, if ever, do hate crimes figure in? INCITE! Women Against Violence is a national activist organization whose mission is to expand the public's social consciousness from narrow definitions of woman-directed violence to include these and other questions. INCITE! distinguishes itself through its two-pronged understanding of violence against women of color, which includes both "'violence directed at communities,' such as police violence, war, and colonialism, and 'violence within communities,' such as rape and domestic violence."

Leading a racial justice movement that posits violence against women within the context of state- and institution-supported forms of violence, INCITE! argues that looking at how women of color experience domestic and sexual violence facilitates understanding how state and institutional violence alter all women's lives. Although specific differences in race, class, gender, and sexuality affect how women experience violence, these factors are rarely present in most conversations on violence against women. Instead, mainstream social service agencies frequently pathologize, or typecast as abnormal, women of color who experience violence and the communities where these acts occur. At the same time, the daily forms of violence to which many women of color are exposed remain overlooked. Take, for example, an undocumented female worker who can face harassment from her family, her community, her employer, and immigration officers all within the same day. In this case, gender, race, and nationality are integrally intertwined. Developing strategies to end these multiple forms of violence requires concurrently addressing each of these factors in ways that can effect change at a larger level. Yet few antiviolence organizations are prepared to do this sort of political organizing.

INCITE! began initially as a conference planned in 2000 in Santa Cruz, California, for women of color antiviolence activists. The event's organizers envisioned collaborating with others who were similarly disillusioned with the lack of intersectional analysis and approach within both racial justice and antiviolence organizations. Although the gathering was intended to remain small, interest in it quickly grew. In all, two thousand women of color attended the conference, and two thousand more were turned away. The enthusiastic response to the participants' unique vision led to a number of offshoot projects. Grassroots chapters and affiliates have been established across the country. The organization has produced two critical anthologies, *Color of Violence: The INCITE! Anthology* and *The Revolution Will Not Be Funded: Beyond the Non-Profit Industrial Complex*, and created a media bureau. In addition, the first conference spawned two more: one in Chicago, "Building a Movement" (2002), and another in New Orleans, "Stopping the War on Women of Color" (2005). The organization also heads several specific issue projects, such as "Stop Law Enforcement Violence," "Policing Sex Work," and "'Quality of Life' Policing." Similarly, INCITE's information-rich website provides numerous fact sheets and position papers on these and other issues. It is also developing a blog forum.

At the heart of INCITE!'s work is its members' belief that by encouraging healing and well-being within communities of color, oppressed individuals stand to grow "closer towards global peace, justice, and liberation." As Nadine Naber, one of the founders of the nearly decade-old organization, puts it, "Part of INCITE!'s framework has to do with not only reacting and critiquing, but trying to think about what would an alternative society that you would want to live in actually look like, and to work towards creating that."

female environment, the Vermont female inmates gained confidence, self-respect, and the necessary peace in their lives to move beyond the bars of their imprisonment. While Vermont's success is an exception to what normally happens to female inmates, it stands as a significant illustration of what can be achieved when a state makes a concerted effort to rehabilitate its prisoners.

Reproductive Rights: Expanding the Options

In 1987, when I was a junior in high school, the Los Angeles Unified School District received funding from a private foundation to establish three school-based health clinics. My high school was one of the three chosen. I remember at the time how much commotion accompanied this decision. For several weeks, whenever we arrived at school or left for the day, we were greeted by picket lines with fist-clenched parents, community members, and local clergy who held signs espousing their rejection of the clinic and urging us to join them. My mother was not among them, but in the crowd I saw my boyfriend's aunt, my friend's dad, and several classmates. One day, I looked up and I saw a skywriting airplane decrying the new center.

These protesters seemed determined to not allow the clinic to open at our school, despite the fact that most of us were Latinos largely from immigrant backgrounds and extremely poor households (about 40 percent of the area's residents still live below the poverty line). And, during the 1980s, San Fernando had one of the worst teenage birth, teen prenatal care, and teen homicide records in all of California. Somehow these protesters managed to hold their impassioned rallies each day with their backs turned away from the daycare center that stood across the street from the campus. Yet whenever I drove into the school parking lot, I could not help but notice the young women my age dutifully depositing their children at the center each morning so they could continue taking classes even though they were now parents. No one ever protested that building.

The clinic has since celebrated its twenty-first anniversary of offering students comprehensive medical care, mental health services, dermatology, health physicals, *and* family planning and pregnancy prevention education. Fears have dissipated and the clinic has proved its usefulness. However, teen pregnancy has not gone away. Neither has the debate about making sex education available to young people. In June 2008, the Centers for Disease Control and Prevention released data that indicated a rise in sex among high school teenagers but a drop in condom use. These figures appear to contradict the Bush administration's aggressive efforts in the first eight years of the 21st century to promote abstinence programs in the United States. An adamant supporter of teen abstinence, Bush repeatedly increased state and federal funding for these programs during his tenure. Even in global aid, Bush stipulated that the HIV/AIDS outreach programs his administration designed include a requirement that one-third of all prevention spending go to abstinence-until-marriage programs. Although they are referred to as the ABC (Abstinence, Be Faithful, and Condoms) programs, condoms and other methods of sexual protection are often left out. In some cases, the countries that receive the funding discourage the distribution of information about sex. In others, it is the United States' insufficient distribution of condoms or commitment to a comprehensive sex education plan that reduces the programs' success.

While mixed approaches such as the ABC programs are potentially ineffective to all recipients, they are particularly dangerous to populations that are economically disadvantaged and at high risk for STIs and pregnancy. For the most part, these problems once again fall along race and class lines. For example, Native American and Alaska Native women are more than five times as likely as white women to contract chlamydia and more than seven times as likely to become infected with syphilis. In addition to claiming an unplanned pregnancy rate that is twice the national average, Latinas are also much more likely than their white female counterparts to contract human papillomavirus (HPV), an infection that can lead to cervical cancer. Similarly, African American women are nearly four times more likely to die in childbirth than white women, twenty-three times more likely to be infected with HIV/AIDS, and fourteen times more likely to die from the disease.

Appalling statistics such as these also carry over into reproductive healthcare. For example, the sharp contrasts in reproductive healthcare between poorer, ethnic communities and mainstream white ones motivated a United Nations committee in 2008 to review the United States' compliance with the International Convention on the Elimination of All Forms of Racial Discrimination (ICERD), a human rights treaty that requires that countries take proactive measures to address racial inequalities. In response to the noncompliance charge, the U.S. government tried to argue that the cited disparities were a result of behavioral choices. However, the UN committee disagreed, noting that government policy plays a much greater role than the United States wants to admit in ensuring that all women have adequate prenatal care, a full range of contraceptive choices, and timely and affordable means to terminating a pregnancy. Similarly, it identified particular problems that prevent women of color from gaining adequate access to reproductive healthcare, including insufficient research on minority women's health, multiple language barriers, the lack of cultural-competency training, and a shortage of minority and women professionals in the reproductive healthcare field.

Ironically, limited reproductive healthcare choices can feed stereotypes that make it seem as if poor women of color who have children or physical disabilities are exploiting governmental social services. Indeed, the argument against welfare fraud is as old as the very concept of public aid. Opponents of public-assistance programs have long argued that these programs are vulnerable to abuse and encourage apathy toward work. However, in the late 1970s, the stigma attached to being a welfare recipient developed a particular face. In his failed 1976 Republican bid for the presidency, Ronald Reagan immortalized the phrase "welfare queen" during one of his campaign speeches in which he told a hyperbolic story about a woman from Chicago's South Side accused of welfare fraud. "She has eighty names, thirty addresses, twelve Social Security cards and is collecting veteran's benefits on four non-existing deceased husbands. And she is collecting Social Security on her cards. She's got Medicaid, getting food stamps, and she is collecting welfare under each of her names," he breathlessly told crowds. The sensationalism of such a charge worked perfectly. So did the racial baiting. Although Reagan never identified the woman, the image of a cheating African American female welfare recipient became a permanent imprint on the American mind.

Women who use state and federal public assistance are regularly regarded with suspicion. They are often accused of draining the country's financial resources while also contributing to its moral corruption. Some interpret their need as laziness and others question whether the money they receive is properly spent. Critics are usually most reproachful when they learn that women have multiple children or are recidivist recipients. In 1996, President Clinton responded to this criticism by signing the Personal Responsibility and Work Opportunity Reconciliation Act (PRWORA), which denies additional benefits to women who have more children while receiving public assistance. Yet neither his administration nor those before or since have adequately addressed the correlation between public assistance and sex education and birth control access. Consequently, acts such as the PRWORA can serve only as punitive measures against low-income women. The 1976 Hyde Amendment, which is still in effect, has had a similar impact. The amendment refuses federal funding of abortions and denies coverage for abortions to military personnel and their families, women receiving care from Indian Health Services, and people on disability insurance. Its passage has also encouraged several state governments to follow suit. To date, thirty-three states have banned funding abortions and thirteen of the seventeen others provide funding only because of court mandates. In essence, these restrictions forfeit the reproductive rights guaranteed by *Roe v. Wade* to low-income women because they limit access. While the Hyde Amendment is at its core tied to the abortion debate, its direct attack on poor women, many of whom are people of color, exposes a racist and class-motivated agenda. In addition, the amendment recalls the United States' long-standing legacy of policing women's bodies.

Eugenics is a form of social engineering that promotes population control as a means of eliminating "negative" traits from the human gene pool. Expanding on his cousin Charles Darwin's "survival of the fittest" theory, Sir Francis Galton is credited with being the first to introduce eugenics into the modern field of science in England in the late 19th century. However, the practice of eugenics stretches across several countries and continents. For example, eugenics was a central premise in Adolf Hitler's *Mein Kampf* and it also helped shape the colonialist discourse that European settlers employed to control Africa. In addition, it was actually in the United States that mass sterilization was first used to pursue "race purification." Theories of social evolution gained popularity during the industrial boom after the U.S. Civil War as one way to address the country's growing social and economic concerns that revolved around issues of race and class. Genetic deviance was blamed for problems such as criminality, poverty, substance abuse, prostitution, and mental illness. Eugenicists argued that removing these genes from the pool would foster a superior human race free of these social ills. However, the implication was that those populations that were believed to carry defective genes had to be eliminated first. Consequently, communities that differed socially or politically from the hegemonic norm were among the most aggressively targeted for population control.

The United States has a long history of sanctioning coercive and nonconsensual sterilizations within communities of color. Sterilization abuse is one of the many methods used through time to control "undesirable" communities. For example, early efforts to contain Native American resistance included germ warfare and rape. African slaves were similarly brought into submission through rape, castration, forced impregnation, and the inability to freely choose sexual partners. During the early 1900s, eugenicists advocated "better breeding" through forced sterilization that combined racial and class prejudices with discrimination against social outcasts. The results were overwhelming. By 1932, more than twenty-six states had passed compulsory sterilization laws that targeted such diverse populations as those who were poor, mentally ill, physically challenged, or incarcerated. The state of North Carolina alone carried out nearly eight thousand sterilizations of supposedly "mentally deficient persons," of whom approximately five thousand were black. In fact, eugenics promoted the notion that pathological behavior could often be traced back to specific racial or ethnic origins. Ultimately, the Nazis' notorious use of eugenics during World War II put an end to the United States' direct association with its philosophies and techniques. However, the debate over rising "unfit" populations continued.

In 1970, the Nixon administration responded to extremist overpopulation fears by establishing federal family planning services aimed specifically at inner city communities. "Population alarmists" linked the previous decade's 25 percent increase in the number of black Americans between the ages of five and nine to the current rise in teen delinquency. This correlation was echoed in 2005 by radio host and former Reagan administration secretary of education Bill Bennett during one of his live shows. Citing the book *Freakonomics*, by Steven D. Levitt and Stephen J. Dubner, Bennett noted, "One of the reasons crime is down is that abortion is up." He then followed up his exchange with a telephone caller by adding, "I do know that it's true that if you wanted to reduce crime, you could—if that were your sole purpose, you could abort every black baby in this country, and your crime rate would go down."

The United States' political ideologies regarding fertility control have also extended beyond its immediate borders. For instance, Puerto Rico, a country that continues to fight against its status as a U.S. territory, has often become a hub for U.S. medical experimentation. Like the Mexican American women in the *Madrigal v. Quilligan* case discussed in the first chapter, Puerto Rican women have been exposed to a series of racist medical practices. As scholar and reproductive rights activist Elena R. Gutiérrez argues in *Undivided Rights: Women of Color Organize for Reproductive Justice*, "Essentially, Puerto Rico and its people have served as a laboratory for American contraceptive policies and products." According to Gutiérrez, contraceptive foams, the IUD, and various forms of the pill were all first tested on Puerto Rican women. In the 1950s, when pharmaceutical companies were

The Relf Sisters

The year 1973 stands as a definitive moment in illustrating the disappointments that the reproductive rights movement has held for women
of color. In January, the U.S. Supreme Court ruling in *Roe v. Wade* gave
women the right to terminate a pregnancy. After a tireless and arduous
crusade, abortion rights activists had succeeded in guaranteeing women
the ability to control their own bodies. However, within the span of only a
few months, this hard-won right proved inconsequential to a set of sisters
from Montgomery, Alabama, who never had the opportunity to exercise
the most important option that the ruling provided women: choice. At ages
fourteen and twelve, Minnie Lee and Mary Alice Relf were sterilized without informed consent by a local hospital operating under orders from the
Family Planning Clinic of the Montgomery Community Action Committee,
which was funded by the U.S. Department of Health, Education and Welfare (HEW). Further inquiry revealed that an additional eleven girls, also
in their teens, had been similarly sterilized in Montgomery. Even more
alarming, the public attention that the Relf sisters' case drew gave way to
the discovery that across the nation between 100,000 and 150,000 people
had been sterilized annually by HEW-funded programs.

Alongside the strides made by the women's movement throughout the
late 1960s and early 1970s, disproportionate numbers of African American, Native American, Puerto Rican, and Chicana women continued to face
sterilization abuse. This issue exposed the sharp differences in women's
experiences due to race and class and revealed some of the conflicts wom-
en of color faced in supporting a feminist agenda. As Angela Davis notes,
"The progressive potential of birth control remains indisputable. But in
actuality, the historical record of this movement leaves much to be desired
in the realm of challenges to racism and class exploitation." The story of
what happened to the Relf sisters reveals the full extent of Davis's point.

In 1971, the Relf family sought assistance from the Montgomery Community Action Committee and was subsequently moved into a public
housing project. Soon after, the mother and her three daughters were
asked to participate in the organization's family planning program. First,
the oldest daughter, Katie, age seventeen, was taken to the Family Planning Clinic where, at the clinic staff's request, she was forced to accept the

insertion of an intrauterine device (IUD). Her mother was not present during this procedure. Then the younger sisters, Minnie Lee and Mary Alice, who were mentally disabled, began receiving Depo-Provera birth control injections, which at the time were still in the experimental stage. In fact, the drug was twenty years away from receiving full approval for public use from the Food and Drug Administration.

As sociologist Thomas Volscho explains in his insightful summary of the case, the turning point came in the summer of 1973. A recent result in the Depo-Provera studies had revealed that the drug caused cancer in lab animals and so the clinic was forced to discontinue the injections. However, because the clinic had been paying for the injections with federal funds, it decided to replace them with sterilization, which was one of the only other birth control methods that HEW funded. Without informing Mrs. Relf of these changes or the plans for the girls' sterilizations, a clinic nurse took Mrs. Relf and her daughters to a local hospital for the procedures. Once there, Mrs. Relf, who was illiterate, was asked to place an "X" on a consent form authorizing the tubal ligations. According to Davis, Mrs. Relf assumed that she was agreeing only to the girls' continued use of the Depo-Provera injections. In fact, the hospital never disclosed the details of the nature of the surgical procedure involved. Mrs. Relf was driven home that night, and the girls were kept overnight at the hospital. The next day, the girls were sterilized and later returned home.

In the aftermath of Minnie Lee and Mary Alice's sterilizations, the Southern Poverty Law Center filed a lawsuit on behalf of the family. *Relf v. Weinberger* (Caspar Weinberger was secretary of the U.S. Department of Health, Education, and Welfare) was decided on March 15, 1974. The district court that heard the case found that in addition to the hundreds of thousands of people sterilized without consent, "Countless others were forced to agree to be sterilized when doctors threatened to terminate their welfare benefits unless they consented to the procedures." Declaring that certain HEW (now called the Department of Health and Human Services) regulations covering sterilizations were "arbitrary and unreasonable," the judge ruled against the use of federal dollars for involuntary sterilizations and the practice of threatening women on welfare with the loss of their benefits if they refused to comply. The attention the Relf case brought to the problem of sterilization abuse was invaluable. Besides Alabama, most

continued

continued from previous page
other states were subsequently forced to reevaluate their medical procedures for women and informed consent has become a standard practice
for all surgical procedures.

The significant differences between the treatment that women of color
and poor white women received in relation to their white, middle-class
counterparts also clarified key factors that distinguished these groups
of women from one another within the reproductive rights movement.
As Davis explains, one of the hesitations that birth control advocates
expressed in supporting an end to sterilization abuse is that it might in-
fringe on the interests of middle-class white women to actually choose
sterilization when they desired it. According to Davis, this revealed the inherent race and class privileges that birth control advocates were unwilling to concede. "While women of color are urged, at every turn, to become
permanently infertile," she argues, "white women enjoying prosperous
economic conditions are urged, by the same forces, to reproduce themselves." With the 1976 Hyde Amendment's being upheld for more than
forty years since its passage, effectively ending poor women's access to
abortion, Davis's critique should not be considered obsolete. The case of
the Relf sisters stands not only as a tragic moment in history for women
of color, but as a reminder of politics that still exist.

banned from conducting medical trials in the continental United
States, they turned to Puerto Rico. Yet for many, the most egregious
example of reproductive rights abuse is the jointly Puerto Rican
and U.S.–sponsored "*operaciones*," which first took place in the late
1930s. Sterilization proponents in the United States capitalized on
Puerto Rico's high birthrates by depicting Latinas as hyperfertile. They
argued that reducing Puerto Rico's population would improve its long-
impoverished economy. With support from Puerto Rico's ruling class
and municipal governments, notes Gutiérrez, hospitals began routinely
performing tubal ligations on women "with consent obtained either
during labor or right after childbirth." Since U.S. federal funding for
contraception was not available in Puerto Rico until 1968 and abortion
was illegal until 1973, *la operación*, as the procedure was commonly
known, became virtually the only birth control choice for Puerto Rican

women. As Gutiérrez reports, "By 1965 about 35 percent of the women in Puerto Rico had been sterilized, two-thirds of them in their 20s."

To redress some of these abuses and ensure against future discriminatory health practices toward Latinas, the National Latina Institute for Reproductive Health (NLIRH) was created in 1994. NLIRH sees itself as a social justice organization dedicated to improving the reproductive health choices for Latinas and "protect[ing] their rights to exercise reproductive freedom." As an advocacy group, NLIRH works to secure adequate funding and health services for Latinas, increase representation of Latina-specific issues within reproductive rights and health policymaking, and guard against exclusionary legal policies that impede the reproductive rights of Latinas and their access to quality healthcare. Operating programs in both policy advocacy and community mobilization, the organization addresses such broad issues as repealing the Hyde Amendment, creating awareness about cervical cancer, incorporating reproductive rights into immigration reform, running leadership training seminars, and serving as an advocacy network. Since its inception, NLIRH has been a leading voice in ensuring reproductive rights and justice for Latinas and forming coalitions with other groups focusing on reproductive health issues as well as with those working more broadly on social justice issues.

The ongoing efforts of organizations such as NLIRH are fundamental to tracking new abuses against women of color. For example, in recent years, poor women of color have continued to be vulnerable to exploitation through the experimentation with hormonal contraception devices such as Depo-Provera and Norplant. Both were marketed as birth control breakthroughs. Administered by a physician every three months, Depo-Provera injections eliminate the need for a woman to rely on daily medication. Similarly, Norplant capsules implanted in the arm to keep women from ovulating provide five years of protection. While these sorts of benefits would seemingly attract a broad range of users, as the editors of *Undivided Rights: Women of Color Organize for Reproductive Justice* note, both drugs were heavily marketed only to Latina, African American, and Native American women. They also continued to be promoted even after reports of dangerous risks and side effects surfaced. Overall, the results of both Depo-Provera and Norplant have been largely negative. In both cases, inconsistent monitoring by the clinics administering them led to many recipients' experiencing severe health problems. Although Depo-Provera is still on the market, Norplant has been discontinued in the United States largely because of the several thousand lawsuits filed against its makers. However, the drug has not disappeared entirely. Most recently, Norplant has been reintroduced in family planning clinics in several developing nations, including Bangladesh, Chile, China, Colombia, Egypt, and Indonesia. Its repercussions on future generations may perhaps only be fully understood through a transnational feminist perspective. Indeed, to grasp the breadth of social injustice against women of color and their acts of resistance in response, one must consider the issue from several different vantage points, including looking across physical borders.

Feminism: Putting Theory into Practice

The integral benefits of applying an intersectional analysis to the social struggles faced by women of color such as health, incarceration, and reproductive rights returns us to the student example I opened with at the beginning of this chapter. When I picked up Jacquelyn's final essay for our community service-learning course, I expected to read an elaboration on the growing pains she had described in class. Instead, Jacquelyn discussed one of the last meetings she had had with the female veterans at her volunteer site. Through time, she and the women had grown friendly with one another. Their talks had grown deeper, although they still teased Jacquelyn about her youth. Finally, Jacquelyn decided to share something with them that changed that. Jacquelyn had grown up in a crack house. As a child, she had watched her mother and her friends regularly snort, smoke, and shoot up. Men came and went, and Jacquelyn was often left to fend for herself. Sometimes she went without food; usually she was left alone. At a certain point, family members intervened and Jacquelyn got the opportunity to lead a more stable life. However, the memories of what she saw and an overall longing for her mother drove her to her own substance abuse. As a teenager, she followed many of the same paths her mother had taken. Although she eventually decided to go a different route, Jacquelyn never underestimated where her earlier life might have taken her. Her desire to pursue feminist course work in college and her interest in working with women attempting to overcome their own demons had never been separate issues for her. It had just taken her a while to find the right voice to articulate them at once.

CHAPTER 4

CREATIVE EXPRESSIONS

CARTOONIST LELA LEE HAS MADE a career out of being angry. It started with getting mad at the Spike and Mike's Sick and Twisted Festival of Animation she attended as a college sophomore. Leaving the controversial yet widely popular film venue, Lee was incensed by the number of racist and misogynist animated shorts that were featured. "I did not enjoy any of those cartoons," she recalled. "They were all making fun of . . . ethnic people, and they were sexist and even though it's a cartoon, it's still not funny to me." Her protracted fuming led a friend to challenge her to create something different. The result was a simple, marker-drawn cartoon she titled "First Day at School." Featuring an outspoken, young female character dubbed the "angry little Asian girl," the short made it clear that Lee was upset by a lot more than the festival.

The cartoon follows her character's arrival at a new school, where she is greeted by a classroom of all-white peers and a clueless teacher who introduces her as an "oriental." After the young girl tells her that the correct term is "Asian," the teacher remarks on her surprisingly "good English." What happens next is now considered a trademark in Lee's early work. A very angry little Asian girl replies, "I was born here, you stupid dipshit! Don't you know anything about immigration? Read some history books, you stupid ignoramus!" Later at home, when her parents confront her about her less than polite comments, the (still) angry little Asian girl looks up from her afternoon snack only to add, "Aw fuck off!"

Although Lee now admits that the angry little Asian girl, whom she has since named Kim, is really a kind of alter ego that allows Lee to speak out against injustice, including that which her own parents often forced her to accept as a child, she was initially embarrassed by the cartoon's content. Consequently, it was not until years later that Lee decided to develop the character. She eventually produced a five-episode video that addressed a variety of anger-inciting issues around being Asian and a woman. In her videos, Lee used the outspoken Kim to discuss such diverse topics as dominant standards of beauty, female sexuality, the model minority myth, and violence against women. Each episode portrayed Kim confronting stereotypes and defying the double passivity typically imposed on Asian women. In particular, her shocking responses refuted not only the immediate situations she faced, but also the history of invisibility and silence that has plagued many women of Asian descent.

In 1998, Lee's collection of shorts made its screen debut, and ironically, Spike and Mike's Sick and Twisted Festival of Animation acquired its exhibition rights. The increased interest in the quirky character led Lee to follow up with a website that featured a weekly comic strip and a line of T-shirts. Even in its early stage, the site received as many as one million visitors in a single month. Lee's angry little Asian girl also sparked mixed reactions among Asians and Asian Americans. Many lauded her efforts to break the stereotype of the quiet, docile Asian woman or the cute Hello Kitty accessory-carrying girl. Others were dismayed by the foul-mouthed language and occasionally crude images. In general, the angry little Asian girl got people talking. However, when Lee decided to venture into making a real profit from her unconventional ideas, she ran into a conflict that many artists of color face when they attempt to break into mainstream popular culture.

Seeking investors and media outlets that might feature her cartoons, Lee was repeatedly turned down because no one believed there was a large enough Asian consumer market. Ultimately, Lee responded by expanding her cast of characters and reintroducing her comic strip as the "angry little girls." Kim now shares the page with Deborah, Maria, Xyla, Wanda, and Pat (a boy). The new characters, whose ethnicities include African American and Latina, are still feisty, but the earlier edgy, sociopolitical commentary has become gradually subdued. In turn, Lee's business has grown exponentially. She is the author of several books, she has put out yearly calendars, and her diversified product line includes purses, dolls, and key chains.

Lee explains her strategic marketing shift as a matter of recognizing that anger about racism and sexism is not limited to Asians. Difference, she notes, can leave many people feeling frustrated and left out. Her comic strip provides an outlet for that. Yet Lee's experience also serves as an example of the obstacles and possibilities that artists of color negotiate when their subject matter is political. For instance, they are often held to expectations from their communities over how to represent their culture and what messages they should project. Similarly, exploring personal issues within their work leaves artists of color open to criticism that they are acting purely from self-interest or personal bias (in contrast to "mainstream" artists, who are presumed bias free). In particular, by not adhering to dominant notions of popular culture, the ethnic content of their work can encounter marginalization. At the same time, within a capitalist economy, artists of color face the pragmatic realization that social relevancy and financial profit sometimes go hand and hand.

Politicizing Pop

While it can be defined in numerous ways, popular culture is usually understood as contemporary cultural expressions that carry mass-market appeal because they engage the broadest audiences possible. Highly influenced by the media, popular culture is also closely tied to capitalism through the vast production of commodities that it encourages. Some people dismiss popular culture for its celebration of the common while others embrace it specifically for its amusement value. In addition, some individuals see popular culture as a critical lens through which to examine the concrete issues that drive our concept of what is deemed superficial in our society.

Take, for example, the effortlessness with which Americans are able to recognize Britney Spears but struggle to name the secretary of state. (Perhaps Hillary Clinton's appointment in the Obama administration will make this answer easier in the future, at least for feminists.) Talking about Britney Spears may not seem immediately political to most people, but examining the multiple power structures that surround her—lawyers, investors, and the fashion industry, to name a few—offers great insight into the politics of race, gender, class, and sexuality that support her name recognition. Similarly, the fact that popular knowledge about Spears supersedes knowledge about actual political matters in our country (and in others, I suspect) underscores the power that comes with capturing the public's consciousness. Some might argue that popular culture can create a numbing effect. For instance, if people are so caught up in tracking a pop star's whereabouts, how likely are they to notice or care about controversial legislative bills or a deteriorating global climate? However, popular culture and "serious" issues are not mutually exclusive, and knowing more about one than the other does not erase the potential for linking the two.

During the 2008 presidential election, Republican candidate John McCain ran several ads using figures such as Spears and Paris Hilton to critique his opponent's popularity. Similarly, both McCain and Barack Obama used various mass media outlets such as MTV, Facebook, and late-night talk shows to boost their appeal. In fact, pop culture became one of their primary sites of battle. Race, class, gender, and sexuality did not remain outside of that struggle either. Incendiary news programs such as those on the Fox television network employed the slang phrase "baby mama" to negatively characterize the frequently forthright Michelle Obama. Used most often to identify a single mother, the term's appropriation into mainstream culture exposed its racist and classist undertones when it was applied to Obama. In a similar manner, a *New Yorker* magazine cover mixing the counterculture image of the 1960s Black Panthers with current musings about Muslims turned a possible satire of the right-wing criticism President Obama received about his cultural background into another form of attack. Indeed, when we consider the powerful role that popular culture plays in shaping current social thought, cultural theorist Stuart Hall's 1981 assertion rings perhaps more true now than ever: "Popular culture is one of the sites where this struggle for and against a culture of the powerful is engaged: it is also the stake to be won or lost in that struggle. It is the arena of consent and resistance."

The double edge of "consent and resistance" in popular culture is largely what makes it such an ambiguous tool of expression for people of color. Ideas and images

This New Yorker *magazine cover, which appeared during the run-up to the 2008 presidential election, mixed imagery from the 1960s Black Power Movement with contemporary ideas about Muslims. Intended as a satire of right-wing criticism of the Obamas, it played on the public's stereotypes and fears.*

about ethnic communities created and circulated by the dominant culture not only serve to establish stereotypes, or what Chicana scholars Mary Romero and Michelle Habell-Pallán call "conceptual blueprints," they are also inevitably a source for rebellion. Lee's angry little Asian girl cartoon subverted the shy lotus blossom "blueprint" that had been drawn out for Asian women by directly addressing this dominant discourse about them. Similarly, many other artists of color have used subculture niches within mainstream outlets to create new visions of their realities.

¡Soy Rasquache y Que!

The term "subculture" can carry negative connotations in that it separates out a group that is identified primarily by its differentiation from the large dominant culture that surrounds it. This places a subculture in the position of being considered tangential, dependent, and often inferior to those in power. Consequently, some cultural theorists reject the term outright. For instance, Alicia Gaspar de Alba prefers understanding Chicano cultural production—or representation—as examples of "alter-Native" perspectives, which emphasize how Chicana/o culture "is not immigrant but native, not foreign but colonized, not alien but different from the overarching hegemony of white America." The relationship to the dominant power structure is still present in reading Chicano culture as alter-Native, but it is not subordinate to it.

Likewise, feminist critic and rhetorician Gwendolyn Pough argues that understanding the meaning and purpose of black subcultures requires contextualizing their evolution in relation *to* the black historical experience in the United States, not despite it. For example, the term "wreck" within hip-hop culture suggests fighting, boasting, or violence. These actions are similar to what many African Americans have had to do in order to be heard or seen within mainstream U.S. society. Consequently, Pough sees black culture as wrecking "in order to obtain and maintain a presence in the larger public sphere, namely, fight hard and bring attention to their skill and right to be in the public sphere."

In 1976, Chicana poet Bernice Zamora proudly reinterpreted the meaning of her marginalization as a stance of resistance against her oppressors: "You insult me / When you say I'm / Schizophrenic. / My divisions are / Infinite." Zamora's words resound with freedom. Refusing to be deemed insignificant or peripheral, the speaker in her poem is unleashed. Indeed, she embodies what Trinh T. Minh-ha calls the "inappropriate other": someone "who moves about with always at least two gestures: that of affirming 'I am like you' while persisting in her difference and that of reminding 'I am different' while unsettling every definition of otherness arrived at." Everything about the speaker in Zamora's poem is inappropriate: She talks back, she embraces a label of ostracism, and she defies marginalization by breaking the logic of artificial boundaries. This rebellious speaker faces multiple oppressions that would likely erase her identity, but she chooses instead to embrace her existence on the fringe as a form of liberation.

Inappropriateness has been a leading trait of mainstream popular culture and is even more pronounced in creative expressions by artists of color. In part, this is tied to the socioeconomic limitations many ethnic communities face. For example, in Mexican and Chicana/o communities, *rasquache* art is art that reimagines the use of inexpensive, commonplace materials that are typically not meant for aesthetic purposes. The religious iconography depicted in calendars hanging from walls in local bakeries and meat markets, the slick low-rider cars thumping along with their decorated hoods, and the black velvet paintings of Aztec scenes that grace the background of many a neighborhood bar are all popular forms of *rasquache* art. As Tomás Ybarra-Frausto, an early observer of *rasquache*'s implicit political nature, puts it, *rasquache* is a "cultural sensibility of the poor and excluded" that "subverts the consumer ethic of mainline culture with strategies of appropriation, reversal, and inversion." In other words, *rasquachismo* inherently turns poverty on its head by creating possibilities from a place of lack. In turn, these creations undermine popular culture's frequent tie to capitalism by relying squarely on what is most readily (and cheaply) available. To borrow from Pough and Trinh respectively, *rasquachismo* "wrecks" difference by "unsettling every definition of otherness."

Several years ago, I was out at a club where the lineup of bands was mainly local, unsigned Chicana and Chicano musicians determined to fuse their political leanings with their love for beats. One group had invested in bumper stickers that not only advertised its name, but that also captured the gist of the attitude that accompanies *rasquachismo*. It read: *¡Soy rasquache y que!* (I'm rasquache and what of it?). Appreciating the implied cheekiness, the crowd went wild for them. I managed to get one and promptly taped it across my office door at work. Every so often, I would notice that someone had tried to peel it off (a *rasquache* move, for sure). Other students, encouraged

Alma López's *Our Lady* (1999)

Artist Alma López's inclusion in the Cyber Arte: Tradition Meets Technology exhibition at the Museum of Folk Art in Santa Fe, New Mexico, seemed simple enough. The 2001 exhibit featured the works of four Latina artists who actively use digital technology to create images that engage traditional cultural iconography. Through its exhibit, the museum hoped to familiarize people with these new technologies and to make visitors more aware of Mexican iconography. Dubbed the "digital diva," López has long explored different interpretations of the Virgin of Guadalupe, one of the most well-known icons in Mexican/Mexican American culture. As a well-established Chicana digital artist, López appeared to be an obvious choice for the exhibit. However, the controversy that followed the display of her work *Our Lady* revealed far more complex issues at hand than just the exploration of familiar images in a new medium. It brought to bear the subtler ways in which gender and sexuality are woven into cultural expectations of creative expression.

Our Lady is a digital print that reimagines the traditional image of the Virgin of Guadalupe. In place of a downcast glance, hands in prayer, and a shapeless figure is a young Latina woman staring directly at her viewers, hands on hips, posing confidently in a bikini of roses. The roses are a direct reference to the Virgin's origin myth; the posture defies the Virgin's traditional submissive stance. In addition, López replaces her trademark blue-and-gold–starred mantle with one that bears the digitally imposed image of Coyolxauhqui, the Aztec moon goddess. This detail reflects the syncretism of Aztec and Catholic religions and recalls the suppression of previous female deities. Rounding out the work is López's replacement of a cherub angel supporting the Virgin from beneath with a bare-breasted woman with butterfly wings, which symbolize the monarch butterfly of López's home state of Michoacán, Mexico. The backdrop of a stage, decorative curtains, and more roses frame the scene.

The Virgin of Guadalupe is considered a manifestation of the Virgin Mary. In addition, she is imbued with several specific cultural symbols that represent the Mexican people. As a mother figure, Our Lady is held in great respect and considered to be a unifying force within the diverse nation of Mexico. For the country's poor, she also represents hope and struggle. As a symbol of femininity, she has long been held as a role model for Mexican women. However, the emphasis on her chastity and submissive state has made her a difficult image to satisfyingly emulate.

The parallels and differences between the traditional representation of the Virgin of Guadalupe and López's are what stand at the heart of the controversy that overtook the museum's digital exhibit. After viewing the print, local community member José Villegas decided to organize a protest to remove it. He argued that López's representation was sacrilegious and insulting. He also claimed possession over the Virgin image, implying that she did not belong to individuals such as López (i.e., queer feminists). In his organizing, he enlisted the assistance of New Mexico Archbishop Michael J. Sheehan, who similarly argued that López's image was indecent in that it represented the Virgin "as a tart or a street woman, not the Mother of God!" The protests surrounding *Our Lady* soon grew hostile, and both López and the museum staff received verbal and physical threats. Nevertheless, the exhibit's curators kept the exhibit intact. In addition, López created a website (www.almalopez.net) to share the thousands of positive and negative responses she received and the various press items that the issue attracted.

In her analysis of López's *Our Lady*, art historian Guisela Latorre notes López's mixed use of "hand-drawn or painted motifs, photography, and preexisting archival/historical material," and adds that "digital media allows López to piece together images from previously fragmented histories in her work." These observations are significant to understanding the feminist importance of López's work. In its traditional form, much of the repressive nature of the Virgin's image goes unquestioned because it has been normalized as a cultural expression of womanhood. However, by altering key elements with other related cultural references and materials, López urges viewers to reconsider the issues of gender and sexuality implicitly attached to an image that is both spiritual *and* cultural. Indeed, there are multiple "histories" underlying the religious image of the Virgin of Guadalupe—histories of indigenous pasts, sexual marginalization, gender violence, racism, and so forth. Acknowledging the presence of these competing histories, López consequently raises the issue of power in representation. As she asks directly in response to the attacks she encountered, "Why do they [the Santa Fe Archdiocese and the protesters] feel more entitled to this cultural icon than the Chicana/Latina/Hispana women in the exhibition?"

by the sign and other Chicana/o-friendly paraphernalia outside my office, occasionally ventured in to say hello and ask about my course offerings.

It escaped me, though, that non-Latino folks might not understand the sticker or its sassiness until one day a colleague from a different department was talking to me and suddenly stopped to ask about it. Caught off guard, I realized it was harder to explain than I thought. I ultimately described it as being akin to "kitsch," but I never felt satisfied with that answer. While it certainly revels in the irreverent, *rasquachismo* is also about defiant invention. It has a pride attached to the resourcefulness in finding a form of expression outside the norm. By bringing together a kind of collage of unrelated elements, *rasquachismo* also demonstrates an ingenuity that can get lost in translation. In addition, as I later realized, in many ways the bond my sticker created between those who walked by and "got it" and myself fostered a type of academic subversion. It established a connection between those "in the know." This exclusion, of course, is what most dominant power structures typically depend on, but here was an example of a "subculture" doing it. We were challenging the blueprint by directly engaging it.

Creating Rage

In her 1981 foundational essay "The Uses of Anger: Women Responding to Racism," Audre Lorde writes, "Women responding to racism is women responding to anger; the anger of exclusion, of unquestioned privilege, of racial distortions, of silence, ill-use, stereotyping, defensiveness, misnaming, betrayal, and co-optation." Twenty-eight years later, many women of color, and black women in particular, find themselves still responding to these problems, only now they must also answer to critiques of the anger they have expelled in addressing them. The stereotype of the angry black woman is a staple in mainstream pop culture. In fact, reality shows such as *The Apprentice* and MTV's *Real World/Road Rules Challenge* got so much leverage out of their two most famous angry black female characters, Omarosa Manigault-Stallworth and Coral Smith, that they brought them back to stir up more trouble in subsequent seasons. Similarly, including a bitchy black antagonist has become almost de rigueur for most films and television series featuring at least one black actress. Consider, for example, how common the sight of a neck-rolling, trash-talking black female supporting character is in contrast to the depiction of a complex, internally conflicted black female lead.

Although one might expect this problem to be the result of an entertainment industry that lacks cultural sensitivity or diversity, projects developed by African Americans fare little better. For instance, despite Mo'Nique's attempts to dispel other stereotypes about black women (her reality shows that address body image and social etiquette deserve some credit), few African American films have cast the actress/comedian in roles in which she is not forced to upbraid one or more of her fellow actors for some insignificant reason. Similarly, who can forget Pam Grier playing the gun-toting, revenge-seeking Coffy in the 1970s blaxploitation films that made her a star? Even earlier, the character of Sapphire Stevens in the television adaptation of *Amos 'n' Andy* that ran from 1951 to 1953 solidified the formulaic role of the quarrelsome, hen-pecking black wife. Whether played for comedic relief or to enhance the dramatic tension, the image of the angry black woman has long overshadowed the actual political rage of black women.

Yet black female artists have endeavored to accurately represent the complexity of their emotions. In her chilling 1939 rendition of "Strange Fruit," Billie Holiday captures both the horror and outrage with which violence against the black community is accepted as naturally as the coming of spring. Singing "Southern trees bear a strange fruit / Blood on the leaves and blood at the root," Holiday's voice reverberates with a stark honesty that met with staunch resistance when she tried to record the song. Fearing financial retaliation for the song's blunt antilynching message, most record producers passed on the option to distribute it. It took Holiday's dogged perseverance and personal investment to finally see it produced. The pain that it brought, however, never quite faded.

While the song eventually became a standard in her repertoire, legend has it that she cried each time after singing it. Holiday's "Strange Fruit" provides us with a glimpse into the depth of emotion that Lorde describes.

Nina Simone's "Mississippi Goddamn" leaves no one guessing about the emotions behind it. Written by Simone in 1963, at the height of the civil rights movement, "Mississippi Goddamn" spells out the final moments of frustration felt by a people faced with an endless string of injustices. Alternating between singing and talking directly to her audience, Simone recounts the numerous sites of offenses: Alabama, where a black church was bombed and four young girls were killed; Tennessee, where the U.S. Commission on Civil Rights met unsuccessfully to address the country's race problems (and where Martin Luther King Jr. was later killed in 1968); and finally, Mississippi, where activist Medgar Evers was gunned down in his driveway while still clutching the NAACP T-shirts he had brought home that night that read JIM CROW MUST GO. Simone's overwhelming response to all these events in succession is the same: Goddamn! Her song unleashes the fury of pain and disappointment at being told to "go slow" and not protest in light of all these assaults. Addressing the rage that is dangerously building up within the community, she bluntly predicts: "Oh but this whole country is full of lies / You're all gonna die and die like flies." Much more than an angry black woman caricature, Nina Simone is the brave messenger of the urgent action required to keep a nation from imploding.

While black women may hold the reigning stereotype, they are certainly not alone in having their passion misconstrued. With their legitimate anger dismissed as evidence of their supposed savagery, Native American women have also struggled to have their protests heard. As scholar Cari Carpenter notes in *Seeing Red: Anger, Sentimentality, and American Indians*, stereotypes of anger have historically served to suppress the resistance of marginalized groups. Arguing that race and gender affect how anger is interpreted, Carpenter sees the expression of anger in Native American women's writing as a response to the denial and loss of human rights. Anger, she contends, is a reaction to a lack of entitlement and is "intimately linked to the possession of self, of land, of nation." Although Carpenter limits most of her discussion to 19th-century Native American writers, her arguments seem equally alive in the works of contemporary artists such as singer and poet Joy Harjo.

In "I Give You Back," from the poetry collection *She Had Some Horses*, Harjo personifies fear as a "beloved and hated twin" who has suppressed her rage against the rape and slaughter of her community. To release it, she finds, she must holistically embrace the multitude of emotions she has previously kept at bay. In particular, she must acknowledge how her justified anger has been displaced by an oppressive fear. Later in the collection, Harjo returns to this theme in the title poem. She describes a woman who possesses "horses." The horses carry scars ("maps drawn of blood"), lack reflection ("threw rocks at glass houses"), act fatalistically ("waited for destruction"), and yet remain vulnerably innocent ("danced in their mothers' arms"). Using these horses as a metaphor, Harjo suggests that her protagonist is kept incapacitated by the feelings that propel her into contradictory, self-destructive actions. To escape this vicious cycle, Harjo's female protagonist must take action. She must get angry. Both in this poem and the former, Harjo lobbies for Native American women to reappropriate the emotions that dominant culture has distorted and to reassume the agency that has been stolen from them. To be free, she proposes, one's anger must be one's own.

Mitsuye Yamada seeks a similar strategy when she urges Asian American women to discourage the invisibility that is frequently imposed on them because of their race and gender. "We must remember that one of the most insidious ways of keeping women and minorities powerless is to let them only talk about harmless and inconsequential subjects, or let them speak freely and not listen to them with serious intent," she argues in an essay in which she discloses her own previous complicity in promoting the image of a quiet, submissive Asian woman. "We need to raise our voices a little more, even as they say to us 'This is so uncharacteristic of you.'" Yamada's point about expectations is what makes the anger expressed by Asian American female artists such

Tracy Chapman

In 1988, a young college grad named Tracy Chapman broke onto the American music scene with a slow-beat, guitar-based song about a woman desperate to escape a lifetime of poverty. Chapman's "Fast Car" was a stark departure from the fun-loving, dance-driven music that defined much of 1980s popular culture. Similarly, its complex treatment of the numerous social problems hindering the poor flew in the face of the era's narcissistic focus on opulence and wealth. Nevertheless, "Fast Car" shot to number 6 on the *Billboard* charts, and Chapman went on to win three Grammys that year, including best new artist, for her self-titled debut album. While some identify Chapman with the folk music movement of the 1960s, others believe she signaled a new direction for the female musicians of her time. In either case, Chapman's presence as an African American woman singing candidly about her working-class experiences defied most notions of what was acceptable to address within mainstream pop and helped usher in a new place for black women in music.

Born in 1964, Chapman grew up in Cleveland, Ohio. A scholarship for disadvantaged youth allowed her to attend Wooster School, a prestigious Connecticut boarding school, which in turn led to her enrollment at Tufts University in Boston. Despite being shy, Chapman became involved in the coffeehouse acoustic music scene as a teenager. In fact, argues musicologist Sheila Whiteley, as Chapman matured intellectually, music became instrumental in exploring her life's experiences vis-à-vis the larger issues facing the nation. "Chapman's personal experience of poverty, racial discrimination and humiliation, together with insights gained on the Boston–Cambridge folk circuit provided a strong grounding for a politicized black woman," explains Whiteley. Chapman herself acknowledged her early awareness of social injustice, penning her first socially conscious song, "Cleveland 78," when she was only fourteen. As she told *Rolling Stone* in a 1988 interview, "As a child, I always had a sense of social conditions and political situations. I think it had a lot to do with the fact that my mother was always discussing things with my sister and me—also because I read a lot."

While Chapman's album was climbing the charts, she began appearing at a number of high-profile political events. Her performance early in 1988 at the Nelson Mandela 70th Birthday Tribute Concert was televised to millions of people around the world. That fall, alongside Bruce Springsteen and Sting, she headlined the Amnesty International Global Rights Now! Tour. Joining several other socially conscious singers such as Natalie Merchant and Michelle Shocked, Chapman also sang at women's festivals across the nation. Each time, she illuminated listeners on a number of significant issues. In songs such as "Why," she questioned the contradictions in supporting expensive missile programs in the name of world peace while ignoring the problems of hunger and violence here in the United States. In others, such as the haunting a cappella "Behind the Walls," she underlined the police's ineffectiveness in responding to domestic abuse.

Many of Chapman's songs also carried a message of urgency. Perhaps most explicitly, in "Talking 'Bout a Revolution," she emphasizes how extreme class inequalities will cause the poor to "rise up and take their share," if those with power do nothing to alleviate the situation. "Better run, run, run . . . / [because] Finally the tables are starting to turn," warns Chapman. These references to the country's mounting racial and class tensions seem particularly prophetic in light of the 1992 Los Angeles riots that occurred soon after.

In her analysis of Chapman's folk-influenced music, Whiteley finds many common ties to rap music, which emerged during the same period. Although they are widely different in delivery, she notes the parallel sentiments and "documentary mode" that both music genres explore. She also emphasizes Chapman's use of other black musical influences such as reggae, blues, and spirituals that many rap artists similarly employ. In addition, as with rap, her socially conscious music has withstood critiques of being "politically angry." Indeed, it is telling that despite Chapman's "willingness to address issues that the U.S. government dismissed during the 1980s: the growing ranks of the homeless, the ever-rising crime rate, and a failing education system," as biographer Jacquelyn L. Jackson writes, she became a household name. Likewise, today Chapman continues to enjoy a devoted following and she has produced several more albums. Mixing in love songs with reflections about the planet, she is still addressing the country's various social issues. In addition, her music has encouraged a new generation of like-minded artists such as Lauryn Hill, Jill Scott, and India Arie who similarly fuse politics with melody. Her most significant achievement, however, remains gaining an international audience to listen and respond to problems that both the Reagan and Bush administrations chose to blindly ignore.

as Lela Lee so provocative. While black and Native American women are criticized for their anger, Asian American women are altogether denied its possession. Imagine then the magnitude of what Kristina Wong accomplishes in her audacious website, Big Bad Chinese Mama .com, when she decides to not just raise her voice but to outright yell.

In addition to her stage performances such as *Wong Flew Over the Cuckoo's Nest,* Wong runs a website that directly confronts the pornographic industry that targets Asian women. Set up as a fake mail-order bride site, Big Bad Chinese Mama addresses the male voyeur seeking "sweet Asian girls." Wong advertises the website in fetish chat rooms and alongside masseuse ads in local newspapers. She also has the site's address linked to search engines so that it comes up when someone is looking for Asian pornography. As Wong explains in the site's "manifesto" section, titled "Resistance as Living: Giving Revolution a Sense of Humor - OR - Why I Tricked Thousands of Nasty Porn Seeking Guys to Come to my Fake Mail Order Bride Site, Only to Get a Fist in Their Face," her decision to create Big Bad Chinese Mama came while she was a student at UCLA. Tired of holding conversations about oppression with everyone but the actual oppressor, and admitting to herself that she was not cut out to be the traditional take-it-to-the streets activist, she chose instead to use humor and the Internet to channel her anger at the popularized image of the pretty, meek Asian girl who also conveniently happens to be an exotic sex vixen. In the process, Wong hoped to initiate a dialogue with the men who seek out this paradoxical cliché.

Wong's site features pictures and biographies of real Asian women who, instead of posing seductively for potential clients as they might in a pornography website, are striking back, literally. They wave fists, kick groins, make ugly faces, and offer more than a few choice words to would-be Asian fetish seekers. In the "FUQ" (frequently unasked questions, acronym pun intended) section, Wong fields questions that male clients would likely ask about Asian mail-order brides. The responses are anything but accommodating or polite. Wong does not hold back in expressing her anger at the sexual perversions that she believes surround the desire for an Asian woman within this context. However, she also uses the opportunity to educate site visitors about other related issues that feed into racist and sexist ideas about Asian women. For instance, in response to "Do your brides speak English?" Wong answers: "You fucking dumbshit. Why wouldn't they speak English? Don't you know that the Asian Diaspora is over 150 years old in America? Not to mention the fact that the fuck faces who designed the education system in America left little room for the multi-cultural experience to thrive and be shared (Sorry, but the lesson plan on the first Thanksgiving doesn't count)."

Like Lee's, Wong's approach to using popular culture to address political topics can have mixed results, and not everyone may see it in a positive light. However, Lee and Wong are both part of a growing number of young Asian American women who are taking suggestions such as Yamada's to heart. They also join others such as comedian Margaret Cho, who broke several barriers when she received her own television program, *American Girl*, in 1994. Cho was unabashedly candid years later when she documented the failure of the series and her subsequent breakdown in *I'm the One That I Want* (1999), a stand-up show (and later book and concert-film) in which she detailed the difficulties she experienced in the entertainment industry because of her weight and ethnicity. Cho's honest admissions, which fluctuate between anger and pain and yet allow for humor, created a forum to publically address the complex experiences of Asian American women specifically, and women of color generally, within greater mainstream culture. They also laid bare the costs of succumbing to such pressures to play the wide-eyed ingenue, the sexy vixen, or the model minority. When Cho released her 2002 show, *Notorious CHO*, in which she addressed her bisexuality, she broke yet another taboo: an admission that not all Asian women are interested in men.

"Casualties of War"

Cho, Wong, Lee, and other Asian American women now bridging the gaps between mainstream pop culture and the creative work produced within their own communities are both indebted and haunted by the women who came before them. Among the most influential was Anna

May Wong, the first Asian American actress to achieve international fame. Wong began her career as a silent film actress with her first leading role at the age of seventeen. She soon transitioned to talking films in which she played a number of supporting roles. A move to Europe brought praise and success along with the promise of better possibilities back in the United States. In fact, after her return, Wong was able to headline several films and eventually even became the first Asian American to star in her own television series, *The Gallery of Madame Liu-Tsong*. However, despite her ambition and the acclaim that followed, Wong became immortalized as the originator of the evil dragon lady in American film, an image that emerged from xenophobic fears about Asians. Having Wong, and later other Asian American actresses, portray the dragon lady on screen allowed Americans to freely exercise their political repulsion of Asian women while simultaneously satisfying their curiosity and sexual attraction for the character's imagined exoticism.

The sexual allure of the dragon lady was fleshed out in the late 1950s when the role of Suzie Wong materialized. Initially a novel, and later adapted for film and stage, *The World of Suzie Wong*, the story of a Chinese hooker with a heart of gold, became an instant sensation. Softer than her dragon lady counterpart, the character of Suzie Wong still maintained her duplicitous nature, but her status as a prostitute made her fair game for any interested male parties. In particular, as the conflicts between the United States and other Asian countries grew, the concept of the naive but experienced Asian sex worker who needed saving from her terrible Asian male oppressors became a household image.

In more recent times, the foreign women of color needing rescue by the United States have become those from the Middle East. Soon after the 9/11 attacks, the Bush administration and the general media began focusing intensely on the oppressive practices against women in Muslim countries. In particular, the expectations for women to cover their hair with veils, or in some cases, wear full body burqas, drew wide criticism and concern. *Beneath the Veil*, a documentary that detailed how women in Afghanistan were prohibited from working, going to school, or being unaccompanied in public first aired on CNN one month before the attacks. At the time, it drew very little interest from the government, the public, or the media. However, when CNN decided to run it twice on September 22 and 23, five-and-one-half million viewers tuned in. In the following days, when Bush pressed Congress for support in the United States's efforts against the Taliban, and later Iraq, he frequently referred to the need to defend women's rights in those countries. Similarly, Feminist Majority Foundation founder and former NOW president Eleanor Smeal posited the attack on the United States in direct relation to the treatment of women in Afghanistan. As she told the *Los Angeles Times*, "These women were the first casualties of the war against the United States."

The United States' vested interest in employing the image of the burqa-clad woman as a symbol for its intervention bears some question. While Muslim countries such as Iraq and Afghanistan are targeted as oppressors, others that maintain profitable relationships with the United States are not. As Maureen Dowd, a columnist for the *New York Times*, asked, "What does it matter if Saudi women can't drive, as long as American women can keep driving their SUVs?" Similarly, why has the United States not taken a more active interest in freeing Muslim women from their religion's oppressive practices in the past? Or, for that matter, what has it done to reduce violence against women at home?

In her graphic novel, and later animated film, *Persepolis*, Marjane Satrapi illustrates her experience as a young adult living in Iran during the country's 1979–1987 revolution. As a result of the Iranian revolution in which the ruling monarch was overthrown, the country was pulled into a long period of widespread repression. Academic institutions were shut down or censored, borders were closed, protesters were either exiled or imprisoned, and women were forced to adopt the veil. Satrapi captures these experiences in a rich narrative that reveals what these changes meant for Iranian women. While she takes a firm stand against the misogyny surrounding the forced use of the veil, she also

© Getty Images/Christopher Furlong

The United States and some other Western nations have positioned themselves as protectors of women in the Middle East. Here, a Muslim woman protests the view that veiling is inherently oppressive.

describes a personally affirming relationship with the Islamic faith. Satrapi's story avoids facile generalizations about Islam and focuses instead on the shortsighted nature of fundamentalism, which leaves no place for intellectual freedom. Consequently, she questions the purpose behind targeting women for their sexuality. Her exploration of Marxism, feminism, and personal agency suggests that Iranian women did not need saving so much as the entire country needed assistance in removing the revolution's corrupt political government, which hid behind distortions of Islam. However, countries such as the United States and Great Britain avoided interfering at the time. The financial ties they had established long ago with Iran and other countries in the surrounding area precluded their involvement. As Satrapi's father, who is portrayed as a loving and supportive man in her works, concludes, "As long as there is oil in the Middle East, we will never have peace."

Publishing from the Margins

Marjane Satrapi's decision to write her own story is not unique. Rather, it is part of the significant and growing body of work by women of color who insist on accurate depictions of their life experiences. The desire to see their culture and history preserved through writing led several women of color in the 1980s to push for their own feminist publishing companies. The earliest of these was Kitchen Table: Women of Color Press, which was based in Boston. Initiated from a conversation between Barbara Smith and Audre Lorde, the collective of feminist and lesbian of color writers and activists who came together in 1980 to found Kitchen Table decided to name it so in order to honor the place in the home where women traditionally gather to work and communicate with one another. They also wanted to emphasize that the press was the creation of working-class women who could not depend on personal wealth or social networking to promote their work. Moreover, they wished to emphasize the marginalization that lesbians of color who were "out" faced in having their work published anywhere.

Intrinsically, the founders of Kitchen Table understood the value in taking control of their image making and not relying on commercial or alternative presses, which were almost all white and male dominated, to get their work published. Until then, women of color were likely to find opportunities for publication only in "special issues" of feminist or literary journals. Their work was characterized simply as supplementary material to other, more important matters. With their work marginalized in this way, the founders of Kitchen Table recognized that they were least likely to reach other women of color through these channels. Establishing their own press in light of the many obstacles they otherwise encountered emphasized the importance their venture brought to bear in expanding social justice. As Smith noted, "Kitchen Table: Women of Color Press is a revolutionary tool because it is one means of empowering society's most dispossessed people, who also have the greatest potential for making change."

Studying Spanish literature several states away in the Midwest during this same time, graduate student Norma Alarcón felt a similar spark of energy. In particular, she was alone and eager to end her isolation. "There weren't enough other women of color or Latinas for me to have a conversation with," she recalled. Alarcón turned to poetry and began seeking out other female writers of color. She then decided to start publishing their work and launched a journal on literature and art. In 1987, Alarcón joined the University of California, Berkeley faculty and brought with her Third Woman Press, with a catalog that grew to include books of fiction, criticism, and poetry. Among its earliest published writers were Sandra Cisneros, Ana Castillo, and Gloria Anzaldúa, all of whom have gone on to become recognizable figures in mainstream publishing and whose literature is frequently taught in classrooms across the United States.

Although Kitchen Table and Third Woman are now defunct, many of the groundbreaking books they produced live on. For example, *This Bridge Called My Back: Radical Writings by Women of Color*, edited by Cherríe Moraga and Gloria Anzaldúa, and published by both presses at different times (Kitchen Table in 1981 and Third Woman in 2002), has gone through three editions and is considered one of the most crucial works to initiate women of color feminist studies. As noted in Chapter 1, *This Bridge* spells out the marginalization that the women of color contributors experienced as writers and feminist thinkers. In addition, it celebrates the multiple strands of their identities. These discussions have evolved and further expanded in subsequent works such as *Making Face, Making Soul/Haciendo Caras: Creative and Critical Perspectives by Feminists of Color* (1990), edited by Gloria Anzaldúa; *This Bridge We Call Home: Radical Visions for Transformation* (2002), edited by Gloria Anzaldúa and AnaLouise Keating; and *Colonize This!: Young Women of Color on Today's Feminism* (2002), edited by Daisy Hernández and Bushra Rehman.

Similarly, *This Bridge* helped encourage the creation of collections that directly address particular ethnic communities or deal with issues related specifically to women of color. For example, *Home Girls: A*

Black Feminist Anthology (1983) collected the work of black lesbian and feminist writers. *Making Waves: An Anthology by and About Asian American Women* (1989) combined fifty-seven critical and creative responses to interrelated discussions on immigration, war, work, family, identity, injustice, and activism. In turn, *Making Waves* gave way to other works such as *Our Feet Walk the Sky: Women of the South Asian Diaspora* (1993), *Dragon Ladies: Asian American Feminists Breathe Fire* (1997), and *YELL-Oh Girls: Emerging Voices Explore Culture, Identity, and Growing Up Asian American* (2001). Similarly, the recent collection *The Color of Violence: The INCITE! Anthology* (2006) by INCITE! Women of Color Against Violence tackles the interrelated struggles that women of color share in response to domestic abuse, sexual assault, and other forms of violence tied to race, class, gender, and sexuality. All of these works can be traced back to *This Bridge* in how they broach the rage and pain that women of color experience in their daily lives with the creative expressions that they use to nevertheless thrive.

The sociopolitical purpose behind Kitchen Table and Third Woman also inspired the development of other small feminist presses. Headquartered in San Francisco, Aunt Lute Books, for example, was founded in 1982 on the principle that it not be "just another white publisher doing women of color." Consequently, the press strove to consciously build a staff that reflected racial, ethnic, and sexual diversity. In 1989, Aunt Lute became a nonprofit organization to have better control over what it published and to fund women from diverse backgrounds to participate in its intern program. During its existence, Aunt Lute has been responsible for producing the first U.S. collection of Filipina/Filipina American women writers and the first collection of Southeast Asian women writers and for bringing numerous translated texts by women from other countries to U.S. readers. Similarly, South End Press, which began operating in 1977, has increasingly focused on creating a fair environment for its workers. Run as a nonprofit collective, it holds each member responsible for core editorial and administrative tasks and pays all collective members the same base salary. To avoid the racial and gender hierarchies that commonly exist in publishing houses, the press has also kept a woman-majority staff since the mid-1980s that has included at least 50 percent people of color since the mid-1990s.

Bodily Expressions

A final aspect to consider in the cultural work produced by women of color is the exploration and use of their bodies as primary sources of inspiration. While histories of exploitation and mistreatment abound, sexuality has also served as a means of expression and empowerment. Many women of color artists have succeeded in reverting the male gaze (through which women are objectified by the way in which men depict them) as well as the subjugating imprint of colonialism by not just acknowledging their sexuality, but also by making it the focus of their creations.

Photographer Laura Aguilar's provocative images are a case in point. Serving as the primary model for her work, Aguilar transforms social expectations of the female nude when she photographs herself. Aguilar is a large woman most would categorize as obese. Conventional wisdom would assume her body is unfit to display and unlikely to evoke an erotic response. However, the freedom Aguilar exacts in her photography has just the opposite effect. In a nature series in which she engages the desert landscape, Aguilar merges her naked body with the open spaces around her. The full roundness of her back becomes a smooth boulder resting against gravel and dirt. The thickness of her breasts and stomach sloped over either side of her body as she stands bent over in a wooded path become earthy mounds of sensual comfort for the woman balanced on her back. With herself as the object, Aguilar undoes her objectification as a woman. As reviewer A. M. Rousseau notes, "[Aguilar] makes public what is most private. By this risky act she transgresses familiar images of representation of the human body and replaces stereotypes with images of self-definition. She reclaims her body for herself." As a Chicana lesbian, Aguilar reclaims in her work a sexuality that is often erased within heteronormative representations of female nudity. Admitting her personal investment in Aguilar's work for the range and complexity of Chicana lesbian desire that it offers, cultural critic Yvonne Yarbro-Bejarano adds, "The desire that flows through [her art] does not limit itself to the sexual: It is for social justice, community, and representation in all its meanings."

Aguilar's photography also recalls the works of other Latinas who have sought to deconstruct shallow sexual stereotypes of Latina women. Cuban American artist Ana Mendieta uses photography, video, sculpture, and performance to capture the symbiotic relationship between women and nature. In several works, she employs mud, sand, and other natural materials to trace her bodily imprint into the landscape. Sometimes, her work

© Laura Aguilar / Courtesy of Los Angeles County Museum of Art

Photographer Laura Aguilar defies expectations about beauty and sexuality by positioning herself in her photographs in unconventional ways. In this image, from the series Stillness, she merges her naked body with the natural open spaces around her.

suggests a peaceful coexistence with her surroundings; at other times, it emphasizes the unnatural violence thrust upon the female body by external forces. Similarly, filmmaker Lourdes Portillo has long captured the joys of sexual awakening alongside the horrors of sexual violence in her work. For example, while Portillo depicts the emerging sexual desire of a Nicaraguan refugee living in San Francisco in *After the Earthquake / Despues del Terremoto* (1979), in *Señorita Extraviada* (2001) she chronicles the sexually linked disappearances and killings of young Mexican women along the United States-Juárez border. Throughout her extensive body of work, Portillo attempts to make politically explicit how the Latina body is treated within the American landscape.

A final artist to consider in her use of the body is Kara Walker, a 1994 winner of the John D. and Catherine T. MacArthur Foundation's "genius" grant and, at age twenty-seven, the award's youngest recipient. Walker is best known for her black paper-cut silhouette depictions of the African American antebellum experience. Employing the 18th-century kitsch art technique, Walker creates dramatic and often disturbing scenes that illustrate the history of African American racial representation. Frequently, for example, she emphasizes images of slavery. The silhouette figures in her work carry children on their backs, engage in community activities, and perform manual acts of labor. Walker purposely pushes the meaning of these anonymous black images. They reveal the realistic and diverse experiences of African American slaves; at the same time, however, their cartoonish shape and the interplay between their black form and the white background against which they are set recall the all-too-familiar ways in which African Americans have been stereotyped and misrepresented. In addition, Walker sets her scenes in fragmented, isolated states that lack clear demarcations. Critics suggest that this approach "invite[s] viewers to fill in the missing elements." Indeed, this direct interaction encourages viewers to recognize the thoughts and emotions that live on in the aftermath of slavery—the various ways in which the United States remains unresolved about its violent past.

Walker has described her experience as an artist as one of gaining control over how she is represented. "There's something about the history of image making that had cast me out," she explains. "Cast me as an object to be viewed or coveted, or seduced or killed, or something other than what I wanted to be or what I thought of myself as." Acknowledging her use of art as a tool to challenge that objectification, she adds, "When you have the ability to make pictures of things, it gives you a sense of possibility." Still, Walker admits that artists of color are often held to expectations that they produce only works that engage issues of race. Otherwise, she notes, critics will suggest that you are not representing yourself accurately. The irony, however, is that these same critics also mistake the range of sentiment that comes with being an artist of color. Engaging the expectations and stereotypes of the angry black woman, Walker only half jokingly comments, "If you are a black artist, you could paint a wall of smiley faces and someone would ask you, 'Why are you so angry?'" Walker's comment echoes the struggles many women of color artists face in not only having their work understood and appreciated, but in being understood themselves, apart from the various assumptions made about their identities as women of color.

CHAPTER 5

LOVING SELVES

LOVE. MY STUDENTS USUALLY LOOK UP from their notes when I start to speak on the topic. Some set down their pencils, assuming love will not be a question on their exams. Most take this moment as a reminder of how our class is different from their other university courses. A class discussion on love makes them curious, suspicious, unsure. Why talk about love now? Where does love fit into the syllabus? This is just an aside, right? But love is central to a course on women of color. It is what has brought me to them, and it is what makes the women we read about and the issues we discuss matter. In addition, love is what provides a way forward for women of color. A love for their well-being and advancement is what will drive future studies about women of color. It is what will fuel the need for future activism. It is what will help future generations define what women of color feminism means to them.

Still, I have to clarify several things before my students and I can actually begin to address love. First, I am not referring to the love associated with candy, flowers, or Hallmark cards. Similarly, while Oprah may be onto something when she brings love into her daily shows, I am also not speaking of a love that can be facilely branded into a book, a film, or a website. The love I am interested in stretches beyond the intimacy of two individuals, although it does involve a deep sense of passion.

Here Is the Love

Writer Audre Lorde refers to the kind of love I want my students to imagine as the power of the erotic. This, too, requires some explanation given the number of distorted perceptions attached to women who dare to claim the erotic as their own. Rather than the superficial banality of pornographic desire by which patriarchy has come to define female sexuality (such as *Girls Gone Wild* or the current infatuation with stripper life), the erotic, as Lorde sees it, is what women have had taken from them that would otherwise be a source of strength, power, and knowledge. Women are traditionally taught to fear the erotic, to interpret the pulse of the emotion it inspires with shame. At the same time, men have used the erotic to control female sexuality, redirecting it so that women believe their sexuality is primarily tied to pleasing men. Encouraged to embrace men as their sole love object, women are often more likely to turn away from one another when they perceive other women as rivals rather than allies. To Lorde, the impact of these losses is simply too great. Self-love and love for and among women, she argues, are vital to our actualization as human beings.

As a lesbian, Lorde has an integral investment in the erotic. The erotic opens up a space of sexual expression and legitimacy that she is invariably denied within a heterosexist patriarchal structure. As a black woman, reclaiming the erotic breaks her free of the histories of racism and abuse attached to black female bodies. And, as a feminist, recuperating the erotic extends her ability to build community with other women. In all, argues Lorde, the erotic promotes a wholeness of self that is difficult to achieve otherwise. In fact, it is this sense of personal fulfillment, she explains, that makes the erotic so powerful and thus threatening. "The erotic is a measure between the beginnings of our sense of self and the chaos of our strongest feelings," she asserts in "Uses of the Erotic: The Erotic as Power." "It is an internal sense of satisfaction to which, once we have experienced it, we know we can aspire. For having experienced the fullness of this depth of feeling and recognizing its power, in honor and self-respect we can require no less of ourselves."

To illustrate what Lorde means, I usually ask students to think back for a moment to an occasion when they experienced a burst of emotion from some act of intimacy. A flutter they felt when they held hands with someone. A tug in their hearts after a first kiss. The hot flush in their faces after the touch of a lover. I ask them to focus on the meaning of that physical feeling and consider the depth of its potency. Then, I have them imagine what it would mean if they could release this concentrated energy source into every part of their lives. At the very least, they would be inspired to create—a picture or a poem, as Lorde suggests, or an amazing term paper, as I joke. More to the point, however, they would feel vitalized, strong, impassioned. Furthermore, they would feel invested in ensuring that this feeling lasts because they would recognize its value as well as their own. This is the power of the erotic.

The idea that we can overcome oppression if we can *feel* the totality of what we are capable of is central to what many women of color feminists theorize as love. While there are concrete and ideological structures that need to be broken down to advance social equality and justice, there is also an emotional repairing that must take place. Racism, sexism, homophobia, and poverty damage our self-esteem and desensitize us to the depths of human emotion. Too often, we relinquish the power we do possess to those oppressors who rely on our emotional deprivation. Not loving others is one of the most effective ways to ensure divisions and internal conflict. Not loving ourselves warrants our annihilation.

As bell hooks writes in *Sisters of the Yam: Black Women and Self-Recovery*, "Love heals." hooks blames the legacy of slavery for much of the psychological damage that the black community has subsequently experienced. The violence and dysfunction that black individuals were forced to adopt as normal, she argues, trained later generations to view love as elusive and settle instead for lesser forms of affection. Too often, these compromises, coupled with feelings of self-hatred and low self-esteem brought on by continued exposure to racism and misogyny in the United States, have led many black women (and many other women of color, I would add) to accept love and abuse as mutual elements in their lives. It is only in undoing this process, insists hooks, that the community can finally be free. Simply enduring is not a good

Sarah Jones's "Revolution"

In 2001, the Federal Communications Committee (FCC) fined KBOO-FM, an Oregon college radio station, $7,000 for an October 1999 airing of actress and poet Sarah Jones's rap poem "Your Revolution." While the song is meant as a feminist critique of the misogyny and commercialism that has overrun rap music in the last two decades, it was misinterpreted by listeners who contacted the FCC complaining that the song was sexually graphic and offensive. The FCC responded by issuing the radio station a citation and banning Jones's song from being played before 10 PM Taken aback by the accusation that the song contained "offensive sexual references" and that those references appear to be designed "to pander and shock and are patently offensive," Jones told *Washington Post* reporter Lonnae O'Neal Parker that she decided to fight the charges to clear her name. In addition, she wanted to make sure that her feminist message, which she shared with such diverse audiences as young high school girls and international women's groups, did not get lost.

"Your Revolution," written in 1997 and inspired by Gil Scott-Heron's "The Revolution Will Not Be Televised," rejects the notion that hip-hop music can objectify and humiliate women and yet still be considered progressive. She reminds the male rappers to whom the song is addressed in its refrain, "Your revolution will not happen between these thighs," and weaves in various references to other rap songs that are in fact much more explicit than hers. Each of these references provides an example of how its singers have forsaken the socially powerful nature of hip-hop in

enough strategy. "Whenever people talk about black women's lives, the emphasis is rarely on transforming society so that we can live fully, it is almost always about applauding how well we have 'survived' despite harsh circumstances or how we can survive in the future," explains hooks. "When we love ourselves, we know that we must do more than survive. We must have the means to live fully. To live fully, black women can no longer deny our need to know love."

Like hooks, writer-activist June Jordan also views love in terms of an impending social movement. To be both black and female, she notes in "Where Is the Love?" is to be forced to necessarily engage in favor of capitalism ("ain't about . . . the Versaces you buys") and the sexual objectification of women ("your revolution will not be you / smackin' it up, flippin' it, or rubbin' it down"). She also takes female rap artists to task, pointing out how their own complicity in this process is equally damaging ("giving up my behind so I can get signed"). Ultimately, Jones concludes, "if we could drop the empty pursuit of props and ego," "the revolution, when it finally comes, is gon' be real."

Although some mistakenly assume that Jones dislikes hip-hop music altogether, she insists it is quite the opposite. "I'm not attacking hip-hop," explains Jones. "I'm attacking sexism in the larger culture. I'm a cultural critic and a member of the hip-hop generation." She also suggests that many musicians sharing her views are "often silenced or driven underground by the corporate rap structure of big record labels and commercial radio stations." Jones's case against the FCC settled in 2003. In her legal briefing, her attorneys noted, "Ms. Jones used the hip-hop vehicle in 'Your Revolution' because she believes it is a beautiful and creative art form. She believes that the appropriate response to the objectionable and disturbing elements in hip-hop is not to walk away from the art form, but to answer back with something more sophisticated and meaningful." As a result of winning her case, "Your Revolution" was removed from U.S. radio stations' "do not play" lists and Jones was able to uphold her First Amendment rights. While Jones has since moved on to doing more stage theater work, her contribution to hip-hop feminism and perseverance to be heard remain powerful gestures.

a struggle against self-negation. The frequent exposure to hatred and contempt that black women encounter requires an "hourly vigilance" to maintaining one's self-love and self-respect—not an easy task in light of the status quo and governing forces that preach otherwise. Yet as Jordan points out, a commitment to love is worthwhile because of its galvanizing opportunity for "all the peoples of the earth." An investment in self-love, self-respect, and self-determination holds the promise of transformation. The majority of the world, she reminds us, is kept powerless through the denial of these qualities. Asking repeatedly, "Where is the love?" Jordan argues that it lies in giving up notions of self-sacrifice and fear. It lies also in rejecting people's attempts to find fulfillment at the expense of another's self-destruction. For Jordan, the goal of a love movement is simple: "I am talking about love, about a deep caring and respect for every other human being, a love that can only derive from secure and positive self-love."

In *Methodology of the Oppressed*, Chela Sandoval reflects on the ability to use love as a mobilizing force. Like Jordan, she finds that the act of "falling in love" can serve as a "conduit" or impetus for the action necessary to challenge oppression. As Sandoval posits, "It is love that can access and guide our theoretical and political *'movidas'* [movements]—revolutionary maneuvers toward decolonized being." Citing several Chicana theorists such as Emma Pérez and Gloria Anzaldúa, Sandoval notes how each of them sees love as an igniting force for social change. In the case of Anzaldúa, it is love that specifically awakens a desire for "crossing over."

In her landmark work, *Borderlands/La Frontera: The New Mestiza*, Anzaldúa describes the duality of being caught between two cultures as a Mexican American, two identities as a Chicana lesbian, and two languages as a bilingual speaker. She defines this multifaceted position that keeps her on the borders of various worlds as a "*mestiza* consciousness" and argues that, rather than reinforcing a reactionary stance against either side, occupying this liminal space encourages one to seek a new location away from conflict. She argues that "the future depends on the straddling of two or more cultures. By creating a new mythos—that is, a change in the way we perceive reality, the way we see ourselves and the ways we behave—la *mestiza* creates a new consciousness. . . . A massive uprooting of dualistic thinking in the individual and collective consciousness is the beginning of a long struggle, but one that could, in our best hopes, bring us to the end of rape, of violence, of war." Anzaldúa imagines men and women, queer and straight, Mexicans and Anglos finding within these borderlands very different ways to treat each other. Their mutual investment will be love. With the *mestiza* as "the officiating priestess at the crossroads," they will come to recognize "*somos una gente* [we are one people]."

Have Love, Will Travel

Philosopher Maria Lugones also joins Anzaldúa in envisioning a journey of cultural understanding that extends across borders. However, as she explains in her thoughtful essay, "Playfulness, 'World'-Travelling, and Loving Perception," that journey can become derailed by a lack of empathy between people and communities. Lugones explains how in order to thrive in a "world" or community a person must feel "normatively happy" within it, meaning that she gladly accepts that world's social norms as her own and is similarly affirmed by them. Such acceptance and affirmation occur in part because the norms are drawn from a common knowledge base within the community. Being able to fully participate in the world also keeps members of a community "humanly bonded" to one another and allows them to build on shared histories.

Consider, for example, the ease with which you move within the "world" you and your closest friends have established together. You have created norms within your circle that reflect your mutual interests, ideas, and beliefs. You have developed your own language and signs. Memories of things you have done together offer you reference points and help you form opportunities for new adventures. Similarly, your shared experiences keep you interconnected, allowing you to regularly renew your affection for each other. Within this world, you exist without question.

Yet Lugones describes the alienation that many women of color feel toward mainstream feminism in terms of its failure to welcome them in "lovingly." Specifically, she notes that the invisibility that women of color feel within dominant white America can be even more pronounced within a white feminist "world." Whereas entry into such a space should be automatic given the fact they are women, many women of color feel as though they are interlopers when they travel into a white feminist world. Lugones argues that this marginalization occurs largely because "white/Anglo" women frequently fail to fully identify with other women "across racial and cultural boundaries." This lack of identification prevents white/Anglo women from developing a loving sense of appreciation for the differences that separate them from women of color. Instead, more often, these differences create feelings of resentment and indifference among white/Anglo women toward women of color. In turn, the "worlds" that white/Anglo women create can reflect this. When women of color enter such spaces, they are unable to create any positive interaction because they are already perceived in ways that have altered their reality as human beings (for example, they are seen as nuisances, considered incapable, or assumed inferior). They remain only objects to reaffirm assumptions about who they are. For example, if they fail at a work task, it confirms that they are less able than their white/Anglo female counterparts. Or if they become emotional, it is because they are inherently illogical. Although unsubstantiated, these conclusions often take a heavy toll on a person's sense of self.

While Lugones believes that women of color can adopt strategies of surviving their trips into these violent worlds by using "playful" methods such as those that lack rules or competition and involve "finding [in] ambiguity and double edges a source of wisdom and delight," she emphasizes that the real goal lies in increasing "cross-cultural and cross-racial loving." Indeed, "playing" is only an intermediate strategy, and there are still many other worlds that women of color enter out of necessity that will always remain hostile. A more consequential answer lies in eliminating the formation of such violent worlds altogether and opening the airways to all travel. When we enter each others' worlds, then, we might be more predisposed to see them through their inhabitants' perspectives. This way of viewing each others' worlds, which is at once intimate and loving because it avoids marginalization by encouraging identification, becomes mutually affirming to both traveler and inhabitant. Similarly, this positive interaction serves as the basis for reinforcing a person's sense of self rather than denying it.

If we return to the example of friendship worlds, we can consider how much deeper and stronger these worlds would be if we assured those outside our friendship circles that they had our empathy. Rather than seeing them as intruders encroaching on our space, we could view them as potential allies, potential colleagues, potential *friends*. Forming these kinds of relationships can only ultimately help us as well. As Lugones emphasizes, "We are fully dependent on each other for the possibility of being understood without which we are not intelligible, we do not make sense, we are not solid, visible, integrated; we are lacking. Travelling to each other's 'worlds' enables us to *be* through *loving* each other."

To Know Me Is to Love Me

In her 2006 essay, "Being Lovingly, Knowingly Ignorant: White Feminism and Women of Color," Mariana Ortega uses Lugones's argument as a framework to survey the current state of love between white feminists and women of color. Specifically, she considers how third wave feminism's commitment to diversity has affected that love. Ortega notes the fervent espousal that this generation of feminists has pledged to significantly addressing race and class alongside gender and sexuality. She also acknowledges these feminists' public cries for inclusion and representation of the marginalized, the women of color. She points to the well-versed white third wave feminist who can effortlessly cite multiple works by women of color and is quick to demonstrate how their ideas reflect her own. Yet, Ortega argues, there is "an ignorance of the thought and experience of women of color that is accompanied by both alleged love for and alleged knowledge about them." In other words, there is a great deal of superficiality to the love and knowledge that many white third wave feminists profess to have for women of color. It is this "loving, knowing ignorance" that most troubles Ortega.

Ortega objects to the ways in which many white feminists will "claim to be concerned about women of color while at the same time being fully engaged in production of ignorance about the lives of these women." She offers several anecdotes as support. Ortega remembers sitting at meetings during which participant after participant encouraged the creation of a space for women of color to speak while she and other women of color sat ignored. She recalls compiling long

Women of Color Blogs

For many years now, interacting across some "worlds" has required only a few broad keystrokes. Through the advent of the Internet and the continuous expansion of the World Wide Web, people have found ways to form links with one another that transcend time, distance, and even language. Drawn to each other by common interests and the desire to communicate, individuals have created forums on websites, electronic social networks, and, in particular, blogs, where they freely share their thoughts and engage in discussing a variety of issues. Women of color are no exception. From developing sites that address sociopolitical topics within their communities to using cyberspace to discuss personal issues, women of color are emerging as a force within the blogging world—and the feminist world. Women of color feminist blogs often feature lively dialogues about political matters affecting communities of color. In addition to offering responses to current events, many of these blogs also provide stories about how the writers experience these issues personally. Blogs by women of color feminists also offer new opportunities for scholars, artists, activists, and other individuals to join in conversations about issues of race, class, gender, and sexuality.

Another common goal uniting many women of color feminist blogs is the ongoing struggle for accurate representation. As scholar-filmmaker and creator of the blog *blac (k) ademic,* which ran from October 2005 to

lists of emerging women of color scholars for a speaking event only to have them discarded in favor of a well-known figure whom everyone had already heard. Most upsetting, she wonders why her experiences and those of her women of color colleagues persist in echoing the frustrations, pains, and disappointments of the oft-cited women of color foremothers.

The visceral nature of Ortega's examples gives me pause. I, too, have experienced this disjunction. I remember preparing to finish my graduate course work and finding myself fortunate enough to have it coincide with a visiting Chicana professor's short stay at my campus. She offered a literary course on feminism of the Américas in which we read several works by authors and theorists I had until then researched

December 2006, Kortney Ryan Ziegler notes, "Our words created progressive images of women of color that contrasted with stereotypical notions of passivity and victimhood. We wrote our own stories because other mainstream blogs tended to ignore, devalue, misrepresent, and neglect the histories, activism, and scholarship of women of color." Empowered by the possibility of enacting change across multiple spaces and locations, bloggers are discovering fresh ways of collaborating and forming alliances. Through their posts and new "cyber-bonds," adds Ziegler, bloggers also disprove the notion that women of color are incapable of contributing to intellectual discourse.

This is not to say that these new forms of outreach and conversation are without occasional tensions. Like any other publishing outlet, the feminist blogging world has seen its own set of controversies (including ones involving the publisher of this book). Debates over plagiarism, exclusion, marginalization, and the disparity in gaining access to other publishing opportunities such as books and magazines show that racism and class bias continue to divide women of color and white feminists. At the same time, blogs with descriptive monikers such as "The Unapologetic Mexican," "Angry Brown Butch," "Reappropriate," and "Diary of an Anxious Black Woman" suggest that the voices of women of color and their conversations with each other and with other groups are only getting louder and stronger, offering hope that the digital airwaves present the possibility for many forms of resolution and community.

only on my own. I was thrilled to finally have an opportunity to engage in a class dialogue about their ideas. However, my mood began to change when the class discussions made me realize that these ideas were so new and foreign to the majority of my peers that most of our time was spent explaining terms, histories, and misconceptions. Their monopoly of the class time and professor thwarted most in-depth discussions of the course materials.

My experiences today are not so different. I remember being heartily congratulated on my tenure promotion the same day another woman of color colleague was denied hers. I recall sitting in a meeting listening to impassioned claims about the need for professors to involve ourselves in the community surrounding our university, yet the suggestion of contributing to a failing local women's shelter servicing a largely women of color population went unobserved. And I cannot forget the dumbfounded look of an invited speaker who, after presenting what she deemed as new feminist scholarship, was surprised by my observation that all of her sources happened to be women of color who had presented these ideas many years before. Ortega's questioning of the sincerity and purpose of efforts to incorporate women of color into contemporary feminism resonates all too strongly. Is knowing their work, claiming to love them, but all the while never really knowing who women of color are or what their experiences mean any better than the explicit marginalization they previously encountered?

Ortega returns to Lugones's travel metaphor for inspiration. She underscores the need for white feminists to reconsider what gaining knowledge about other women means. Traveling to someone's world should "include learning her language, living in her environment, trying to understand issues from her perspective (as hard as this may be), and imagining what it means to be her in her 'world.'" Not having this mutual exchange takes us back to what W. E. B. DuBois described experiencing when he spoke of an African American double consciousness. The marginalized know their own worlds as well as the mainstream world. However, those people in the "center" worlds tend to know little about the worlds that exist on the margins, as bell hooks also indicates.

Ortega's suggestions offer a way to put an end to these harmful forms of alienation from one another. For example, we can apply her concepts of travel and understanding to the particular struggles that women of color seeking an education face that their white/Anglo female counterparts might not. Adapting to the kind of critical writing and speaking skills required in an academic setting can mean for women of color the extra task of learning to express themselves in a language other than their own native tongue. Juggling the stresses of school life might include also having to care for family at home. Having few or no classmates and professors who resemble them can be extremely isolating to women of color. Returning home to an environment that has little understanding or appreciation for education can feel discouraging to women of color. If those occupying dominant worlds within academia fully understood and had empathy for these differences, women of color might have higher educational success rates, and eventually these differences might altogether fall away. The process can only begin, however, by initiating a sincere attempt to travel, as Ortega argues.

Indeed, we must remain mindful of how oppression is replicated and avoid dehumanization at all costs. As Barbara Smith once reminded an audience, "Feminism is the political theory and practice that struggles to free *all* women: women of color, working-class women, poor women, disabled women, lesbians, old women—as well as white, economically privileged, heterosexual women. Anything less than this vision of total freedom is not feminism, but merely female self-aggrandizement." This kind of concrete basis for empathy and the shared experiences of traveling into each other's worlds open up the possibility of real growth within the feminist movement because at the heart of it is actual love.

Loving Abroad

To take the metaphor of world traveling a bit further, it is important as we discuss the future of women of color feminism to move beyond domestic travel. Transnational feminism opens up the borders of academic study and activism in that it requires traveling globally to gain a mutual understanding of the worlds of women and the connections between women elsewhere and women here in the United States. In many ways, this process signals the need for extending the love project sketched out by the women discussed in this chapter. Loving, empathetic traveling becomes especially salient when we consider the acceleration with which U.S. women of color and women in third world nations become subject to the same systems of economic and gender exploitation as countries grow more globally intertwined. For example, the similarities between the rising number of sex tourism cases in the Caribbean and the sexual assaults that women experience as they attempt to migrate across the U.S.-Mexico border are so great that we must discuss them in relation to one another. Similarly, a brief glance at the women working in domestic labor across U.S. homes today reveals that the once familiar faces of African American, Puerto Rican, and Mexican women serving as nannies and maids to white American families are giving way to those of women from places as diverse as Central America, the Philippines, and Africa, reflecting recent immigration patterns.

In their anthology *Global Woman: Nannies, Maids and Sex Workers in the New Economy*, editors Barbara Ehrenreich and Arlie Russell Hochschild note that one of the more significant factors that link women from poor countries with those in first world nations is their increasingly shared presence in the workforce. For first world women, "the absence of help from male partners" has led those who wish to or must work outside the home to "turn over the care of their children, elderly parents, and homes to women from the Third World." For third world female migrant workers, the need to support their children, parents, and extended families, coupled with the lack of economic opportunities in their own countries, has forced them to travel across thousands of miles, often enduring life-threatening conditions, to take care of other women's families and homes.

Despite the striking gender shifts in the global workforce ("half of the world's 120 million legal and illegal migrants are now believed to be women"), the editors argue that the experiences of female migrant workers remain understudied or unacknowledged because of their severe marginalization within the first world. For example, because many are women of color, they are perforce "subject to the racial 'discounting'" in countries where their presence has already established them as a permanent underclass (e.g., Mexicans in the United States, Asians in the United Kingdom). In addition, the "private 'indoor' nature" of their work, which usually takes place in homes, keeps them hidden from public view. In the case of sex workers, the illegal activity involved in their profession leaves them even more isolated. Finally, another reason that Ehrenreich and Hochschild give for the lack of knowledge about the fate of female migrant workers curiously returns us to the relationship that they share with first world women. Ehrenreich and Hochschild posit that the pressure "affluent careerwomen" in the United States feel to succeed at "doing it all" (e.g., "producing a full-time career, thriving children, a contented spouse, and a well-managed home") lead them to "preserve the illusion" by keeping their domestic help out of sight. They note that what wealthy countries seem more interested in extracting from third world countries today is not only the natural resources and agricultural products that they have long exported, but "something that can look very much like love."

Defining Worlds

In recognizing the growing significance of transnational feminist studies, it is important to also take a moment to reflect on the boundaries implicit in continuing the use of the term "women of color." The concept of women of color exists most tangibly within the margins of the U.S. experience. As discussed in Chapter 1, the construction of race is tied largely to the invisible privileges attached to whiteness. The term "women of color" helps us define a group, however diverse, of female individuals who collectively experience disempowerment because they lack access to these privileges as a result of their race/ethnicity, class, and gender. The term is also helpful in identifying similarly sustained patterns of resistance to and subversion of these barriers. However, women of color come from communities that are not always categorically U.S. based. Likewise, neither are their experiences. In fact, many factors such as immigration, violence, and reproductive rights require analyses that reach across geographical borders. Indeed, Native Americans and people of African, Caribbean, Latin American, and Asian descent living in the United States are tied both in culture and sociopolitical experiences to many communities outside the United States. For these reasons, the term "women of color" is sometimes limited in addressing the experiences of the women to whom it refers.

In recent years, there has been a move to more directly link women of color studies to transnational or global feminisms. For example, in their essay "Transnational Practices and Interdisciplinary Feminist

Scholarship: Reconfiguring Women's and Gender Studies," Caren Kaplan and Inderpal Grewal urge readers to rethink the notion of U.S. women of color as a singular unit, or what they call a "homogenized figure of racialized and sexualized difference." They argue instead that women's studies consider examining women's experiences across nations or "transnationally" in order to address the "globalized inequities" that mutually underpin their oppressions.

Yet redirecting the feminist focus to emphasize internationalism over the domestic also runs the risk of once again avoiding responsibility and discussion of the internal factors that create the specific experiences of women of color living in the United States, as Chicana feminist Sandra Soto counters in "Where in the Transnational World are U.S. Women of Color?" Or, as in her essay "Locating Global Feminisms Elsewhere: Braiding US Women of Color and Transnational Feminisms," Elora Halim Chowdhury thoughtfully adds, "While there are important points of intersection between histories and struggles of US women of color and third world women, and therefore potential for powerful alliances, collapsing the two in to one category smudges over the necessity of analyses around nation as well as race." Indeed, while there are several different considerations to assess, at the very least, divergent perspectives such as these and others indicate that women of color as a field of study is at a crossroads and that the issues that women within and outside the United States face are enmeshed in significant and recurrent ways.

Future Lovers

The similarities and needs between women across nations, including our own, reinforce why we must put our love and commitment into nurturing a future generation of feminists. Many new challenges are in front of us and many more other challenges are still unresolved. As our worlds grow ever more interconnected, the answers can lie only in strengthening the bridges with our sisters across the ways. Indeed, we need to recognize how much needs to get done as much as how much potential we have to be the ones to do it. The compelling collection of essays by young women of color, *Colonize This! Young Women of Color on Today's Feminism*, edited by Daisy Hernández and Bushra Rehman, ends with the words of a young hip-hop feminist, Shani Jamila, who wisely reminds us, "The most important thing we can do as a generation is to see our new positions as power and weapons to be used strategically in the struggle rather than as spoils of war. Because this shit is far from finished." By the time my students have read their last assignment, finished their exams, and set their pencils down for the last time in my class, I hope that they, too, realize this. They are our "worlds'" next caretakers and lovers.

READER'S GUIDE

Questions for Discussion

In what ways do you feel that you are in control of how people perceive you? What assumptions get made about you based on your race, ethnicity, and gender? Do you think that these assumptions affect how you are able to live your life or what you are able to accomplish? Do you ever use stereotypes or shorthand racial information when encountering someone for the first time? If so, why?

Name three recent negative portrayals of women of color in the media. What stereotypes and historical images do each of these portrayals rely on? Describe three positive portrayals of women of color you have encountered recently. What made them positive?

What are some of the effects of colonialism and slavery that you encounter in your daily life? How do these affect you? How do you respond to them?

In what ways do you think feminism today addresses issues relevant to women of color? In what ways do you think it falls short? Do you think feminism is a good vehicle for women of color to seek and achieve justice and equality, or do you think other movements are more promising? Why?

Why is intersectionality important when addressing feminist issues faced by women of color?

What are some ways you can incorporate feminist theory into concrete practice?

Does your family or community use any forms of cultural expression that are outside the mainstream dominant culture? If so, how are they useful in challenging dominant norms of gender, class, and cultural expectations?

What popular culture idioms or sayings do you find offensive and why? For these idioms, propose new ways of using language that is empowering and revolutionary.

Do you think third wave feminism differs from second wave feminism in its approach to race, ethnicity, and class? If so, how?

Do you think love has political potential? Why or why not? Do you think a politician could successfully include love in her or his platform? What might this look like?

Topics for Research

Social Issues

Pick a social issue that affects women of color (for example, education, domestic violence, employment, immigration). How do the experiences of women of color differ from those of white women? How do they differ from those of men of color? How has feminism approached this issue? In what ways has feminism addressed—or failed to address— the intersections of race, class, ethnicity, sexuality, and gender as they pertain to this issue? Through what other movements or mechanisms have women of color worked on this issue?

Local Activism

Research an organization in your community that is working to improve the lives of women of color. When was the group formed? What issues is it addressing? What are its goals? What tactics is it using to achieve them? Is it working in coalition with other groups? If so, which ones? If it is providing services, how does it do its outreach? Who provides funding?

Creative Expression

Research two or three women artists or performers who create or represent alternative images for girls and women of color. How do these women and their work challenge and contest dominant depictions of women's bodies and their sexuality? How does their work upend mainstream assumptions and stereotypes based on race, ethnicity, class, gender, and/or sexuality? How has their work been received by the mainstream media and/or public?

FURTHER READING AND RESOURCES

BOOKS

Alaniz, Yolanda, and Nellie Wong. *Voices of Color.* Seattle: Red Letter, 1999.

Alarcón, Norma, ed. *Chicana Critical Issues.* Berkeley, CA: Third Woman, 1993.

Alvarez, Julia. *In the Time of Butterflies.* New York: Plume, 1995.

Anzaldúa, Gloria. *Borderlands/La Frontera: The New Mestiza.* San Francisco: Aunt Lute, 1987.

———. *Making Face, Making Soul/Haciendo Caras: Creative and Critical Perspectives by Feminists of Color.* San Francisco: Aunt Lute Foundation, 1990.

Anzaldúa, Gloria, and AnaLouise Keating, eds. *This Bridge We Call Home: Radical Visions for Transformation.* New York: Routledge, 2002.

Arrizón, Alicia. *Queering Mestizaje: Transculturation and Performance.* Ann Arbor: University of Michigan, 2006.

Asian Women United of California. *Making Waves: An Anthology of Writings by and About Asian American Women* (3rd ed.). Beacon, 1989.

Athey, Stephanie, ed. *Sharpened Edge: Women of Color, Resistance, and Writing.* Westport, CT: Praeger, 2003.

Bambara, Toni Cade. *Salt Eaters.* New York: Random House, 1980.

Behar, Ruth, and Deborah A. Gordon, eds. *Women Writing Culture.* Berkeley: University of California, 1995.

Bhavnani, Kum-Kum, ed. *Feminism and "Race."* New York: Oxford University, 2001.

Bobo, Jacqueline, ed. *Black Feminist Cultural Criticism.* Malden, MA: Blackwell, 2001.

Bow, Leslie. *Betrayal and Other Acts of Subversion: Feminism, Sexual Politics, Asian American Women's Literature.* Princeton, NJ: Princeton University, 2001.

Browdy de Hernández, Jennifer, et al. *Women Writing Resistance: Essays on Latin America and the Caribbean.* Boston: South End, 2004.

Cantú, Norma, and Olga Nájera-Ramírez. *Chicana Traditions: Continuity and Change.* Urbana and Chicago: University of Illinois, 2002.

Caraway, Nancie. *Segregated Sisterhood: Racism and the Politics of American Feminism.* Knoxville: University of Tennessee, 1991.

Castillo, Ana. *Massacre of the Dreamers: Essays on Xicanisma.* Albuquerque: University of New Mexico, 1994.

Chancy, Myriam J.A. *The Scorpion's Claw.* United Kingdom: Peepal Tree, 2004.

Chow, Esther Ngan-ling, Doris Y. Wilkinson, and Maxine Baca Zinn. *Race, Class, and Gender: Common Bonds, Different Voices.* Thousand Oaks, CA: Sage, 1996.

Christian, Barbara. *Black Feminist Criticism: Perspectives on Black Women Writers.* New York: Pergamon, 1985.

Cole, Johnnetta B. *All American Women: Lines That Divide, Ties That Bind.* New York: Free Press, 1986.

Cole, Johnnetta B., and Beverly Guy-Sheftall. *Gender Talk: The Struggle for Women's Equality in African American Communities.* New York: Ballantine, 2003.

Collins, Patricia Hill. *Black Feminist Thought: Knowledge, Consciousness, and the Politics of Empowerment.* New York: Routledge, 1991.

———. *From Black Power to Hip Hop: Racism, Nationalism, and Feminism.* Philadelphia: Temple University, 2006.

Comwell, Anita. *Black Lesbian in White America.* Tallahassee, FL: Naiad, 1983.

Crow Dog, Mary. *Lakota Woman.* New York: Grove Weidenfeld, 1990.

Dandicat, Edwidge. *Breath, Eyes, Memory.* New York: Vintage, 1998.

Das Gupta, Monisha. *Unruly Immigrants: Rights, Activism, and Transnational South Asian Politics in the United States.* Durham, NC: Duke University, 2006.

Davis, Angela. *Women, Race, and Class.* New York: Random House, 1981.

de Jesus, Melinda L., ed. *Pinay Power: Peminist Critical Theory: Theorizing the Filipina/American Experience.* New York: Routledge, 2005.

de la Torre, Adela, and Beatríz M. Pesquera, eds. *Building with Our Hands: New Directions in Chicana Studies.* Berkeley and Los Angeles: University of California, 1993.

Donaldson, Laura E. *Decolonizing Feminisms: Race, Gender, and Empire Building.* Chapel Hill: University of North Carolina, 1992.

Enloe, Cynthia. *Bananas, Beaches and Bases: Making Feminist Sense of International Politics.* Berkeley: University of California, 2001.

Enns, Carolyn Zerbe, and Ada L. Sinacore, eds. *Teaching and Social Justice: Integrating Multicultural and Feminist Theories in the Classroom.* Washington, DC: American Psychological Association, 2004.

Esquibel, Catrióna Rueda. *With Her Machete in Her Hand: Reading Chicana Lesbians.* Austin: University of Texas, 2006.

Findlen, Barbara, ed. *Listen Up: Voices from the Next Feminist Generation.* Seattle, WA: Seal, 2001.

Fountas, Angela Jane, ed. *Waking Up American: Coming of Age Biculturally.* Emeryville, CA: Seal, 2005.

Fusco, Coco. *The Bodies That Were Not Ours: And Other Writings.* London and New York: Routledge, 2001.

Galang, M. Evelina. *Her Wild American Self: Short Stories.* Minneapolis, MN: Coffee House, 1996.

———. *One Tribe: A Novel.* Kalamazoo: New Issues Western Michigan University, 2006.

Garcia, Alma M., ed. *Chicana Feminist Thought: The Basic Historical Writings.* New York: Routledge, 1997.

Gaspar de Alba, Alicia. *Sor Juana's Second Dream: A Novel.* Albuquerque: University of New Mexico, 1999.

Giddings, Paula. *When and Where I Enter: The Impact of Black Women on Race and Sex in America.* New York: W. Morrow, 1984.

Gillis, Stacy, Gillian Howie, and Rebecca Munford, eds. *Third Wave Feminism: A Critical Exploration.* New York: Palgrave Macmillan, 2004.

Guy-Sheftall, Beverly. *Words of Fire: An Anthology of African-American Feminist Thought.* New York: The New Press, 1995.

Gutiérrez, Elena R. *Fertile Matters: The Politics of Mexican-Origin Women's Reproduction.* Austin: University of Texas, 2008.

Harris, Laura. *Notes from a Welfare Queen in the Ivory Tower: Poetry, Fiction, Letters and Essays.* New York: Face to Face, 2002.

Hernández, Daisy, and Bushra Rehman. *Colonize This! Young Women of Color on Today's Feminism.* New York: Seal, 2002.

Him, Chanrithy. *When Broken Glass Floats: Growing Up Under the Khmer Rouge, a Memoir.* New York: W. W. Norton, 2001.

Hodges, Graham Russell. *Anna May Wong: From Laundryman's Daughter to Hollywood Legend.* New York: Palgrave Macmillan, 2005.

Hoeveler, Diane Long, and Janet K. Boles, eds. *Women of Color: Defining the Issues, Hearing the Voices.* Westport, CT: Greenwood, 2001.

Hoffman, Eva. *Lost in Translation: A Life in a New Language.* New York: E. P. Dutton, 1990.

hooks, bell. *Ain't I a Woman: Black Women and Feminism.* Boston: South End, 1981.

———. *Feminism Is for Everybody: Passionate Politics.* Boston: South End, 2000.

———. *Salvation: Black People and Love.* New York: Perennial, 2001.

———. *Talking Back: Thinking Feminist. Thinking Black.* Boston: South End, 1989.

———. *Yearning: Race, Gender, and Cultural Politics.* Boston: South End, 1990.

Houck, Davis W., and David E. Houck, eds. *Women and the Civil Rights Movement, 1954–1965.* Jackson: University Press of Mississippi, 2009.

Hull, Gloria T., Patricia Dell Scott, and Barbara Smith, eds. *All the Women Are White, All the Blacks Are Men, But Some of Us Are Brave: Black Women's Studies.* Old Westbury, NY: Feminist, 1982.

Hune, Shirley, and Gail M. Nomura, eds. *Asian/Pacific Islander American Women: A Historical Anthology.* New York: New York University, 2003.

Hurston, Zora Neale. *Their Eyes Were Watching God: A Novel.* New York: J. B. Lippincott, 1937.

Hurtado, Aída. *Voicing Chicana Feminisms: Young Women Speak Out on Sexuality and Identity.* New York: New York University, 2003.

Husain, Sarah, ed. *Voices of Resistance: Muslim Women on War, Faith and Sexuality.* Emeryville, CA: Seal, 2006.

Ige, Barbara K., and María Ochoa, eds. *Shout Out: Women of Color Respond to Violence.* Emeryville, CA: Seal, 2007.

INCITE! Women of Color Against Violence. *Color of Violence: The INCITE! Anthology.* Cambridge, MA: South End, 2006.

Jacobs, Harriet A. *Incidents in the Life of a Slave Girl: Written by Herself [1861].* Edited by Jean Fagan Yellin. Cambridge, MA, and London: Harvard University, 1987.

James, Stanlie M., and Abena P. A. Busia, eds. *Theorizing Black Feminisms: The Visionary Pragmatism of Black Women.* New York: Routledge, 1993.

Jones, Gayl. *Corregidora.* New York: Random House, 1975.

Kadi, Joanna. *Thinking Class: Sketches from a Cultural Worker.* Boston: South End, 1996.

Katrak, Ketu H. *Politics of the Female Body: Postcolonial Women Writers of the Third World.* New Brunswick, NJ: Rutgers University, 2006.

Kaye/Kantrowitz, Melanie. *The Colors of Jews: Racial Politics and Radical Diasporism.* Bloomington: Indiana University, 2007.

Khazzoom, Loolwa, ed. *Flying Camel: Essays on Identity by Women of North African and Middle Eastern Jewish Heritage.* New York: Seal, 2003.

Kim, Elaine, H. Lilia V. Villanueva, and Asian Women United of California, eds. *Making More Waves: New Writing by Asian American Women.* Boston: Beacon, 1997.

Kincaid, Jamaica. *Annie John.* New York: Farrar, Straus, and Giroux, 1995.

Lahiri, Jhumpa. *Unaccustomed Earth.* New York: Random House, 2008.

Larsen, Nella. *Passing.* New York: Arno, 1969.

Latina Feminist Group. *Telling to Live: Latina Feminist Testimonios.* Durham, NC: Duke University, 2001.

Lee, Janet, and Susan M. Shaw. *Women's Voices, Feminist Visions: Classic and Contemporary Readings.* Mountain View, CA: Mayfield, 2001.

Lee, Rachel C. *The Americas of Asian American Literature: Gendered Fictions of Nation and Transnation.* Princeton, NJ: Princeton University, 1999.

Lorde, Audre. *Zami: A New Spelling of My Name.* Trumansberg, NY: Crossing, 1983.

Louie, Miriam Ching Yoon. *Sweatshop Warriors: Immigrant Women Workers Take on the Global Factory.* Boston: South End, 2001.

Marshall, Paule. *Brown Girl, Brownstones.* Old Westbury, NY: Feminist Press, 1959.

Matsuda, Mari. *Where Is Your Body? And Other Essays on Race, Gender, and the Law.* Boston: Beacon, 1996.

Menchú, Rigoberta. *I, Rigoberta Menchú: An Indian Woman in Guatemala.* London: Verso, 1984.

Mohanty, Chandra Talpade. *Feminism Without Borders: Decolonizing Theory, Practicing Solidarity.* Durham, NC: Duke University, 2004.

Mohanty, Chandra Talpade, Robin L. Riley, and Minnie Bruce Pratt. *Feminism and War: Confronting US Imperialism.* London: Zed, 2008.

Molinary, Rosie. *Hijas Americanas.* Emeryville, CA: Seal, 2007.

Morgan, Joan. *When Chickenheads Come Home to Roost: My Life as a Hip-Hop Feminist.* New York: Simon and Schuster, 1999.

Morrison, Toni. *A Mercy.* New York: Alfred A. Knopf, 2008.

———. *Beloved.* New York: Alfred Knopf, 1987.

———. *Playing in the Dark: Whiteness and the Literary Imagination.* Cambridge, MA: Harvard University, 1992.

———. *Sula.* New York: Alfred Knopf, 1973.

Nam, Vickie, ed. *YELL-Oh Girls! Emerging Voices Explore Culture, Identity, and Growing Up Asian American.* New York: Harper Collins, 2001.

Naylor, Gloria. *Bailey's Cafe.* New York: Harcourt Brace Jovanovich, 1992.

———. *Mama Day.* New York: Ticknor and Fields, 1988.

Nelson, Jennifer. *Women of Color and the Reproductive Rights Movement.* New York: New York University, 2003.

Niemann, Yolanda Flores, et al., eds. *Chicana Leadership: The Frontiers Reader.* University of Nebraska, 2002.

Nouraie-Simone, Fereshteh, ed. *On Shifting Ground: Muslim Women in the Global Era.* New York: Feminist Press, 2005.

Nunez, Elizabeth, and Jennifer Sparrow, eds. *Stories from Blue Latitudes: Caribbean Women Writers at Home and Abroad.* Emeryville, CA: Seal, 2006.

Nye, Naomi Shihab. *19 Varieties of Gazelle: Poems of the Middle East.* New York: Greenwillow, 2002.

Pérez, Domino Renee. *There Was a Woman: La Llorona from Folklore to Popular Culture.* Austin: University of Texas, 2008.

Perez, Emma. *The Decolonial Imaginary: Writing Chicanas in History.* Bloomington: Indiana University, 1999.

Pernal, Mary. *Explorations in Contemporary Feminist Literature: The Battle Against Oppression for Writers of Color, Lesbian and Transgender Communities.* New York: Peter Lang, 2002.

Ruiz, Vicki, with Ellen Carol DuBois, eds. *Unequal Sisters: An Inclusive Reader in U.S. Women's History* (4th ed.). New York: Routledge, 2007.

Sandoval, Anna Marie. *Toward a Latina Feminism of the Americas: Repression and Resistance in Chicana aand Mexicana Literature.* Austin: University of Texas, 2008.

Segura, Denise A., and Patricia Zavella, eds. *Women and Migration in the U.S.-Mexico Borderlands.* Durham, NC: Duke University, 2007.

Shah, Sonia, ed. *Dragon Ladies: Asian American Feminists Breathe Fire.* Boston: South End, 1997.

Shange, Ntozake. *Sassafrass, Cypress, and Indigo: A Novel.* New York: St. Martin's, 1982.

Shimizu, Celine Parreñas. *The Hypersexuality of Race: Performing Asian/American Women on Screen and Scene.* Durham, NC: Duke University, 2007.

Siegel, Deborah. *Sisterhood, Interrupted: From Radical Women to Grrls Gone Wild.* New York: Palgrave Macmillan, 2007.

Silko, Leslie Marmon. *Ceremony.* New York: Viking, 1977.

Silliman, Jael, et al. *Undivided Rights: Women of Color Organize for Reproductive Justice.* Cambridge, MA: South End, 2004.

Silliman, Jael, and Ynestra King, eds. *Dangerous Intersections: Feminist Perspectives on Population, Environment, and Development*. Cambridge, MA: South End, 1999.

Smith, Barbara. *Home Girls: A Black Feminist Anthology*. New Brunswick, NJ: Rutgers University, 2000.

Smith, Valerie. *Not Just Race, Not Just Gender: Black Feminist Readings*. New York: Routledge, 1998.

Solomon, Irvin D. *Feminism and Black Activism in Contemporary America: An Ideological Assessment*. Westport, CT: Greenwood, 1989.

Stanley, Sandra Kumamoto, ed. *Other Sisterhoods: Literary Theory and U.S. Women of Color*. Urbana and Chicago: University of Illinois, 1998.

Stetz, Margaret D., and Bonnie B. C. Oh. *Legacies of the Comfort Women of World War II*. Armonk, NY: M.E. Sharpe, 2001.

Tumang, Patricia Justine, and Jenesha de Rivera, eds. *Homelands: Women's Journeys Across Race, Place, and Time*. Emeryville, CA: Seal, 2006.

Twine, Frances Winddance, and Kathleen M. Blee, eds. *Feminism and Antiracism: International Struggles for Justice*. New York: New York University, 2001.

Walker, Alice. *In Search of Our Mothers' Gardens: Womanist Prose*. New York: Harcourt Brace Jovanovich, 1983.

———. *The Color Purple*. New York: Harcourt Brace Jovanovich, 1982.

Weitz, Rose. *The Politics of Women's Bodies: Sexuality, Appearance, and Behavior*. New York: Oxford University, 1998.

White, E. Frances. *Dark Continent of Our Bodies: Black Feminism and the Politics of Respectability*. Philadelphia: Temple University, 2001.

Williams, Patricia J. *The Alchemy of Race and Rights*. Cambridge, MA: Harvard University, 2003.

Wing, Adrien K., ed. *Critical Race Feminism: A Reader*. New York: New York University, 1997.

Women of South Asian Descent Collective. *Our Feet Walk the Sky: Women of the South Asian Diaspora*. San Francisco: Aunt Lute, 1998.

Wong, Jade Snow. *Fifth Chinese Daughter*. New York: Harper, 1950.

Young, Gay, and Bette Dickerson. *Color, Class and Country: Experiences of Gender*. London: Zed, 1994.

Yuh, Ji-yeon. *Beyond the Shadow of Camptown: Korean Military Brides in America*. New York: New York University, 2004.

Yung, Judy. *Unbound Feet: A Social History of Chinese Women in San Francisco*. Berkeley: University of California, 1995.

FILMS

After the Earthquake / Despues Del Terremoto. Directed by Lourdes Portillo and Nina Serrano. American Film Institute, 2003.

The Black List: Volume One. Directed by Timothy Greenfield-Sanders. Perfect Day Films, 2008.

The Black List: Volume Two. Directed by Timothy Greenfield-Sanders. Freemind Ventures, 2008.

Black Women in the Civil Rights Movement. C-SPAN, National Cable Satellite Corp., 2006.

Chicana. Directed by Sylvia Morales. Sylvan Productions, 1989.

Cho Revolution. Written by Margaret Cho. Directed by Lorene Machado. Wellspring Media, 2004.

Corpus: A Home Movie for Selena. Directed by Lourdes Portillo. Xochitl Films, 1999.

Daughters of the Dust. Directed by Julie Dash. Kino International, 1999.

Edge of Each Other's Battles, The: The Vision of Audre Lorde. Directed by Jennifer Abod. Women Make Movies, 2000.

The Grace Lee Project. Directed by Grace Lee. Women Make Movies, 2005.

Halving the Bones. Directed by Ruth L. Ozeki. Women Make Movies, distributor, 1995.

Ida B. Wells: A Passion for Justice [The American Experience]. Directed by William Greaves. California Newsreel, 2004.

Imitation of Life. Directed by Douglas Sirk. Universal International Pictures, 1959.

Leslie Marmon Silko. Directed by Matteo Bellinelli. Films for the Humanities, 1995.

Made in L.A / Hecho en Los Angeles. Directed by Almudena Carracedo. California Newsreel, 2007.

Miss India Georgia. Directed by Daniel Friedman and Sharon Grimberg. Urban Life Productions, 1997.

Mitsuye and Nellie, Asian-American Poets. Directed by Mitsuye Yamada and Nellie Wong. Women Make Movies, 1981.

Passion for Justice, A. Directed by William Greaves. California Newsreel, 1989.

Saving Face. Directed by Alice Wu. Sony Pictures, 2005.

Señorita Extraviada. Directed by Lourdes Portillo. Women Make Movies, 2001.

Slaying the Dragon. Directed by Deborah Gee and Herb Wong. National Asian American Telecommunications Association, 1995.

Still Revolutionaries. Directed by Sienna McLean. Department of Communication, Stanford University, 2000.

Straightlaced: How Gender's Got Us All Tied Up. Directed by Debra Chasnoff. Groundspark, 2009.

Toni Morrison: A Writer's Work. Directed by Gail Pellett. Films for the Humanities and Sciences, 1994.

Towelhead. Directed by Alan Ball. Indian Paintbrush, 2007.

Watermelon Woman. Directed by Cheryl Dunye. Dancing Girl, 1996.

Women of Hope: Latinas Abriendo Camino. Directed by Maria Peralta and Moe Foner. Films for the Humanities and Sciences, 2004.

Yuri Kochiyama: Passion for Justice. Directed by Patricia Saunders and Rea Tajiri. National Asian American Telecommunications Association, 1997.

WEBSITES

African-American Women Online Archival Collections: http://library.duke.edu /specialcollections/collections/digitized/african-american-women

American Indian Women: A Research Guide: http://frank.mtsu.edu/~kmiddlet/history /women/wh-indn.html

Asian Communities for Reproductive Justice: www.reproductivejustice.org

Asian Immigrant Women Advocates: www.aiwa.org/index.php

Blackgirl International: www.blackgirl.org

Black Women for Reproductive Justice: www.bwrj.org

Black Women's Health Imperative: www.blackwomenshealth.org

California Latinas for Reproductive Justice: www.californialatinas.org

Center for the Study and Research of African Women in Cinema: www.africanwomen incinema.org/AFWC/Home.html

CLNET Chicana Studies: http://clnet.sscnet.ucla.edu/women/womenHP.html

Coerced Sterilization of Native American Women: www.geocities.com/capitolhill/9118 /mike.html

Coloredgirls.com: www.coloredgirls.com

GABRIELA Network: www.gabnet.org

INCITE! Women of Color Against Violence: www.incite-national.org

Khmer Girls in Action: http://kgalb.org

Latina Lista: www.latinalista.net/palabrafinal

Latinitas: www.latinitasmagazine.com

Making Face, Making Soul: A Chicana Feminist Website: www.chicanas.com

National Asian Women's Health Organization: http://nawho.org

National Indian Women's Health Resource Center: www.niwhrc.org

National Latina Health Network: www.nlhn.net

Proyecto Latina: http://proyectolatinachicago.blogspot.com

Racialicious: www.racialicious.com

Sahki for South Asian Women: www.sakhi.org

Sister Song: Women of Color Reproductive Health Collective: www.sistersong.net

Third Wave Foundation: http://thirdwavefoundation.org

VG/Voices from the Gaps: Women Artists and Writers of Color: http://voices.cla.umn .edu

Women and Prison: A Site for Resistance: www.womenandprison.org

Women of Color United: www.womenofcolorunited.org

Women of Color, Women of Words: African American Female Playwrights: www.scils .rutgers.edu/~cybers/home.html

Women's Prison Association: www.wpaonline.org

SOURCES

Prologue

Kaye/Kantrowitz, Melanie. *The Color of Jews: Racial Politics and Radical Diasporism.* Bloomington: Indiana University, 2007.

Lee, Rachel. "Notes from the (Non)Field: Teaching and Theorizing Women of Color." In Robyn Wiegman, ed., *Women's Studies on Its Own.* Durham, NC: Duke University, 2002, pp. 82–105.

Wideman, John Edgar. *Fatheralong: A Meditation of Fathers and Sons, Race and Society.* New York: Vintage, 1995.

Chapter 1
"Identity Is the Bane of Subjectivity's Existence"

Espino, Virginia. "'Woman Sterilized as Gives Birth': Forced Sterilization and Chicana Resistance in the 1970s." In Vicki Ruiz, ed., *Las Obreras: Chicana Politics of Work and Family.* Los Angeles: UCLA Chicano Studies Research Center, 2000, pp. 65–81.

Gutiérrez, Elena R. *Fertile Matters: The Politics of Mexican-Origin Women's Reproduction.* Austin: University of Texas, 2008.

Madrigal v. Quilligan. 1978. United States District Court. No. CV 74-2057-JWC. May 30.

Smith, Sidonie. "Identity's Body." In Kathleen Ashley, Leigh Gilmore, and Gerald Peters, eds., *Autobiography and Postmodernism.* Amherst: University of Massachusetts, 1994, pp. 266–292.

"A Peculiar Sensation"

Collins, Patricia Hill. "The Social Construction of Black Feminist Thought." In Joy James and T. Denean Sharpley-Whiting, eds., *The Black Feminist Reader.* Malden, MA: Blackwell, 2000, pp. 183–207.

DuBois, W. E. B. *The Souls of Black Folk.* New York: Cosimo, 2007 [originally published 1903].

hooks, bell. *Feminist Theory: From Margin to Center.* Boston: South End, 1984.

Lorde, Audre. "Age, Race, Class, and Sex: Women Redefining Difference." In *Sister Outsider: Essays and Speeches*. Freedom, CA: The Crossing, 1984, pp. 114–123.

Trinh, T. Minh-ha. "Not You/Like You: Post-Colonial Women and the Interlocking Questions of Identity and Difference." In Gloria Anzaldúa, ed., *Making Face, Making Soul/Haciendo Caras: Creative and Critical Perspectives by Women of Color*. San Francisco: Aunt Lute, 1990, pp. 371–375.

"White Like Me"

Lorde, Audre. "Age, Race, Class, and Sex: Women Redefining Difference." In *Sister Outsider: Essays and Speeches*. Freedom, CA: The Crossing, 1984, pp. 114–123.

McIntosh, Peggy. "White Privilege: Unpacking the Invisible Knapsack." *Independent School*, 49.2, 1990, pp. 31–36.

Morrison, Toni. *Playing in the Dark: Whiteness and the Literary Imagination*. Cambridge, MA: Harvard University, 1992, pp. 9–10.

Murphy, Eddie. "White Like Me." *Saturday Night Live*, December 15, 1984, season 10, episode 9.

Safire, William. "On Language; People of Color." *New York Times*, November 20, 1988, p. 18.

Identity Nations

Mohanty, Chandra Talpade. "Cartographies of Struggle: Third World Women and the Politics of Feminism." In Chandra Talpade Mohanty, Ann Russo, and Lourdes Torres, eds., *Third World Women and the Politics of Feminism*. Bloomington: Indiana University, 1991, pp. 1–47.

Muñoz, Carlos, Jr. *Youth, Identity, Power: The Chicano Movement*. San Francisco: Verso, 1989.

Wei, William. *The Asian American Movement*. Atlanta: Temple University, 1993.

Conflicting Alliances

Allen, Paula Gunn. *The Sacred Hoop: Recovering the Feminine in American Indian Traditions*. Boston: Beacon, 1986.

Brown, Elaine. *A Taste of Power: A Black Woman's Story*. New York: Pantheon, 1992.

Chabram Dernersesian, Angie. "And, Yes . . . The Earth Did Part: On the Splitting of Chicana/o Subjectivity." In Adela de la Torre and Beatríz M. Pesquera, eds., *Building with Our Hands: New Directions in Chicana Studies*. Berkeley: University of California, 1993, pp. 34–56.

Crenshaw, Kimberlé. "Mapping the Margins: Intersectionality, Identity Politics, and Violence Against Women of Color." *Stanford Law Review*, 43.6, 1991, pp. 1241–1299.

Ling, Susie. "The Mountain Movers: Asian American Women's Movement in Los Angeles." *Amerasia Journal*, 15.1, 1989, pp. 51–67.

Mihesuah, Devon A. "Commonalty of Difference: American Indian Women and History." *American Indian Quarterly*, 20.1, 1996, pp. 15–27.

Moraga, Cherríe. *Loving in the War Years: Lo Que Nunca Pasó por Sus Labios*. Boston: South End, 1983, pp. 90–144.

Still Revolutionaries. Directed by Sienna McLean. Department of Communication, Stanford University, 2000.

Bridging Identities

Anzaldúa, Gloria. *Borderlands/La Frontera: The New Mestiza*. San Francisco: Aunt Lute, 1987.

Armstrong, Elisabeth. *The Retreat from Organization: U.S. Feminism Reconceptualized*. New York: SUNY, 2002.

Bambara, Toni Cade. "Foreword." In Cherríe Moraga and Gloria Anzaldúa, eds., *This Bridge Called My Back: Writings by Radical Women of Color*. New York: Kitchen Table, 1983, pp. vi–viii.

Lorde, Audre. *I Am Your Sister: Black Women Organizing Across Sexualities*. New York: Kitchen Table, 1985.

Moraga, Cherríe. *Heroes and Saints & Other Plays*. Albuquerque: West End Press, 1994, pp. 1–35.

Moraga, Cherríe, and Gloria Anzaldúa, eds. *This Bridge Called My Back: Writings by Radical Women of Color*. New York: Kitchen Table, 1983.

Smith, Barbara, and Beverly Smith. "Across the Kitchen Table: A Sister-to-Sister Dialogue." In Cherríe Moraga and Gloria Anzaldúa, eds., *This Bridge Called My Back: Writings by Radical Women of Color*. New York: Kitchen Table, 1983, pp. 113–127.

Black People Love Us

Black People Love Us! www.blackpeopleloveus.com. Accessed July 2, 2009.

Ogunnaike, Lola. "Black-White Harmony: Are You Kidding Me?" *New York Times*, November 17, 2002, p. 11.

Washington, Robin. "The Color of Funny: Racially Based Humor Depends on Who's Doing the Joking." *Boston Herald*, March 17, 2003, p. 37.

Anna Mae Pictou-Aquash

Cannon, Angie. "Healing Old Wounds." *U.S. News and World Report*, 135.22, December 22, 2003, pp. 34–39.

Davey, Monica. "Member of Indian Movement Is Found Guilty in 1975 Killing." *New York Times*, February 7, 2004, p. A11.

Mihesuah, Devon A. *Indigenous American Women: Decolonization, Empowerment, Activism*. Lincoln: University of Nebraska, 2003.

Chapter 2

Brown, Elaine. *A Taste of Power: A Black Woman's Story*. New York: Pantheon Books, 1992.

Donna Summer. www.donnasummer.com. Accessed July 2, 2009.

"Donna Summer." *Wikipedia.* http://en.wikipedia.org/wiki/Donna_Summer. Accessed July 2, 2009.

Huey, Steve. "Donna Summer: Biography." All Music. www.allmusic.com/cg/amg .dll?p=amg&sql=11:kiftxqr5ldae. Accessed July 2, 2009.

Kutulas, Judy. "'You Probably Think This Song Is About You': 1970s Women's Music from Carole King to the Disco Divas." In Sherrie A. Inness, ed., *Disco Divas: Women and Popular Culture in the 1970s.* Philadelphia: University of Pennsylvania, 2003, pp. 172–194.

Shakur, Assata. *Assata: An Autobiography.* Chicago: Lawrence Hill, 2001.

Legacies of the Past

Davis, Angela. "Reflections on the Black Woman's Roles in the Community of Slaves." *Black Scholar,* 3, 1971, pp. 2–15.

Hine, Darlene Clark. "Rape and the Inner Lives of Black Women in the Middle West: Preliminary Thoughts on the Culture of Dissemblance." In Ellen Carol DuBois and Vicki L. Ruiz, eds., *Unequal Sisters.* New York and London: Routledge, 1990, pp. 292–297.

Pilgrim, David. "Jezebel Stereotype." Big Rapids, MI: Jim Crow Museum of Racist Memorabilia, Ferris State University. www.ferris.edu/htmls/news/jimcrow/jezebel. Accessed July 3, 2009.

———. "The Mammy Caricature." Big Rapids, MI: Jim Crow Museum of Racist Memorabilia, Ferris State University. www.ferris.edu/htmls/news/jimcrow/mammies. Accessed July 3, 2009.

Rawick, George P., ed. *The American Slave: A Composite Autobiography.* Westport, CT: Greenwood, 1972.

Turner, Patricia A. *Ceramic Uncles and Celluloid Mammies: Black Images and Their Influence on Culture.* New York: Anchor, 1994.

The Politics of Sexuality

Collins, Patricia Hill. *Black Sexual Politics: African Americans, Gender, and the New Racism.* New York: Routledge, 2005.

Combahee River Collective. "A Black Feminist Statement." In Cherríe Moraga and Gloria Anzaldúa, eds., *This Bridge Called My Back: Writings by Radical Women of Color.* New York: Kitchen Table, 1983.

Pollard-Terry, Gayle. "For African American Rape Victims, a Culture of Silence." *Los Angeles Times,* July 20, 2004, p. E1.

Robinson, Lori S. *I Will Survive: The African-American Guide to Healing from Sexual Assault and Abuse.* New York: Seal, 2002.

Colonizing Bodies

Green, Rayna. "The Pocahontas Perplex: The Image of Indian Women in American Culture." *Massachusetts Review,* 16.4, 1975, pp. 698–714.

Pocahontas. Directed by Michael Gabriel and Eric Goldberg. Walt Disney Feature Animation, 1995.

Smith, Andrea. *Conquest: Sexual Violence and American Indian Genocide*. Boston: South End, 2005.

Body Counts

Allen, Paula Gunn. *The Sacred Hoop: Recovering the Feminine in American Indian Traditions*. Boston: Beacon, 1986.

Fears, Darryl, and Kari Lydersen. "Native American Women Face High Rape Rate, Report Says." *Washington Post,* April 26, 2007, p. A14.

Pan, Esther. "Medicine Wheel." *Washington Monthly,* 32.1–2, 2000, pp. 26–30.

Smith, Andrea. *Conquest: Sexual Violence and American Indian Genocide*. Boston: South End, 2005.

Fatherly Fallacies

Aguilar-San Juan, Karin. "Foreword: Breathing Fire, Confronting Power, and Other Necessary Acts of Resistance." In Sonia Shah, ed., *Dragon Ladies: Asian American Feminists Breathe Fire*. Boston: South End,1997, pp. ix–xi.

"A History of Japanese Americans in California: Immigration." *Five Views: An Ethnic Historic Site Survey for California.* www.nps.gov/history/history/online_books/5views/5views4a.htm. Accessed July 3, 2009.

Allen, Paula Gunn. *The Sacred Hoop: Recovering the Feminine in American Indian Traditions*. Boston: Beacon, 1986.

Cordova, Dorothy. "Voices from the Past: Why They Came." In Asian Women United of California, ed., *Making Waves: An Anthology of Writings by and About Asian American Women*. Boston: Beacon, 1989, pp. 42–49.

First Blood. Directed by Ted Kotcheff. Orion Pictures, 1982.

Full Metal Jacket. Directed by Stanley Kubrick. Warner Brothers, 1987.

Moran, Rachel F. *Interracial Intimacy: The Regulation of Race and Romance*. Chicago: University of Chicago, 2003.

Okihiro, Gary Y. *Margins and Mainstreams: Asians in American History and Culture*. Seattle: University of Washington, 1994.

Perdue, Theda. "Cherokee Women and the Trail of Tears." In Vicki Ruiz and Ellen Carol DuBois, eds., *Unequal Sisters* (3rd ed.). New York: Routledge, 2000, pp. 93–104.

Said, Edward. *Orientalism*. New York: Vintage, 1979.

Shah, Sonia. "Introduction: Slaying the Dragon Lady: Toward an Asian American Feminism." In Sonia Shah, ed., *Dragon Ladies: Asian American Feminists Breathe Fire*. Boston: South End, 1997, pp. xii–xxi.

Volpp, Leti. "(Mis)Identifying Culture: Asian Women and the 'Cultural Defense.'" In Jean Yu-wen Shen Wu and Min Song, eds., *Asian American Studies: A Reader*. New York: Rutgers University, 2000, pp. 391–422.

Warrier, Sujata. *(Un)heard Voices: Domestic Violence in the Asian American Community.*

San Francisco: Family Violence Prevention Fund [pamphlet, n.d.]. http://fvpfstore
.stores.yahoo.net/unvoicdomvio.html. Accessed July 3, 2009.

Yamada, Mitsuye. "Invisibility Is an Unnatural Disaster: Reflections of an Asian
American Woman." In Cherríe Moraga and Gloria Anzaldúa, eds., *This Bridge Called
My Back: Writings by Radical Women of Color* (2nd ed.) New York: Kitchen Table,
1983, pp. 35–40.

Yim, Sun Bin. "Korean Immigrant Women in Early Twentieth-Century America." In
Asian Women United of California, ed., *Making Waves: An Anthology of Writings by
and About Asian American Women.* Boston: Beacon, 1989, pp. 50–60.

Yung, Judy. "Unbound Feet: Chinese Women in the Public Sphere." In Vicki Ruiz and Ellen
Carol DuBois, eds., *Unequal Sisters* (3rd ed.). New York: Routledge, 2000, pp. 257–267.

"So Many Gay All Over the World"

Candelaria, Cordelia. "La Malinche, Feminist Prototype." *Frontiers: A Journal of Women's
Studies,* 5.2, 1980, pp. 1–6.

Cisneros, Sandra. "Guadalupe the Sex Goddess." In Ana Castillo, ed., *Goddess of the
Americas: Writings of the Virgin of Guadalupe.* New York: Riverhead, 1996, pp. 46–51.

Fregoso, Rosa Linda. *MeXicana Encounters: The Making of Social Identities on the
Borderlands.* Berkeley: University of California, 2003.

I'm the One That I Want. Written by Margaret Cho. Directed by Lionel Coleman. Cho
Taussig Productions, 2000.

Paz, Octavio. "Sons of La Malinche." *The Labyrinth of Solitude and Other Writings.* New
York: Grove, 1961, pp. 65–88.

Rich, Adrienne. "Compulsory Heterosexuality and Lesbian Existence." In Henry
Abelove, Michele Barale, and David Halperin, eds., *The Lesbian and Gay Studies
Reader.* New York: Routledge, 1993, pp. 227–254.

Señorita Extraviada. Directed by Lourdes Portillo. Women Make Movies, 2001.

Trujillo, Carla. "Chicana Lesbians: Fear and Loathing in the Chicano Community." In
Norma Alarcón, et al., *Chicana Critical Issues.* Berkeley, CA: Third Woman, 1993,
pp. 117–125.

Hottentot Venus

Gilman, Sander L. *Difference and Pathology: Stereotypes of Sexuality, Race, and Madness.*
(2nd ed.). New York: Cornell University, 1985.

Holmes, Rachel. *African Queen: The Real Life of the Hottentot Venus.* New York: Random
House, 2007.

Yellow Woman

Allen, Paula Gunn. *The Sacred Hoop: Recovering the Feminine in American Indian
Traditions.* Boston: Beacon, 1986.

Silko, Leslie Marmon. *Storyteller.* New York: Arcarde, 1981.

———. *Yellow Woman.* Melody Graulich, ed. New Brunswick, NJ: Rutgers University,
1993.

————. *Yellow Woman and a Beauty of the Spirit*. New York: Simon and Schuster, 1997.

Korean Camptown Women

Lee, Amy, and Joseph Tse-Hei Lee. "Korean Military Brides in New York." *Inter-Asia Cultural Studies*, 8.3, 2007, pp. 458–465.

Park, Soo-mee. "Former Sex Workers in Fight for Compensation." *JoongAng Daily*, October 30, 2008. http://joongangdaily.joins.com/article/view.asp?aid=2896741. Accessed July 3, 2009.

Yuh, Ji-Yeon. "Out of the Shadows: Camptown Women, Military Brides and Korean (American) Communities." *Hitting Critical Mass*, 6.1, 1999, pp. 13–33.

Josefa Loaiza

Rojas, Maythee. "Josefa Segovia." In Cordelia Candelaria, Peter Garcia, and Arturo Aldama, eds., *Encyclopedia of Latino Popular Culture* (vol. 1). Westport, CT: Greenwood, 2004, pp. 750–751.

————. "Re-membering Josefa: Reading the Mexican Female Body in California Gold Rush Chronicles." *WSQ: Women Studies Quarterly*, 35.1–2, 2007, pp. 126–148.

Chapter 3

Davis, Angela Y. *Women, Race and Class*. New York: Random House, 1981.

Health: Healing Against the Odds

Amusa, Malena. "Asian Women Face 'Model Minority' Pressures." *Women's eNews*, September 18, 2006. www.womensenews.org/article.cfm?aid=2891. Accessed July 3, 2009.

Augustine, Jennifer. "Young Women of Color and the HIV Epidemic." Advocates for Youth, January 2003. www.advocatesforyouth.org/index.php?option=com_content&task=view&id=466&Itemid=177. Accessed July 3, 2009.

Benson, Heidi. "Historian Iris Chang Won Many Battles: The War She Lost Raged Within." *San Francisco Chronicle*, April 17, 2005, p. CM-4.

Bradshaw, Carla K. "Asian and Asian American Women: Historical and Political Considerations in Psychotherapy." In Lillian Comas-Díaz and Beverly Greene, eds., *Women of Color: Integrating Ethnic and Gender Identities in Psychotherapy*. New York: Guilford, 1994, pp. 72–113.

Brooks, Siobhan. "Black Feminism in Everyday Life: Race, Mental Illness, Poverty and Motherhood." In Daisy Hernández and Bushra Rehman, eds., *Colonize This! Young Women of Color on Today's Feminism*. New York: Seal, 2002, pp. 99–118.

Cohen, Elizabeth. "Push to Achieve Tied to Suicide in Asian-American Women." *CNN.com*, May 16, 2007. www.cnn.com/2007/HEALTH/05/16/asian.suicides/index.html. Accessed July 3, 2009.

Coridan, Cathi, and Cara O'Connell. *Meeting the Challenge: Ending Treatment Disparities for Women of Color*. Alexandria, VA: National Mental Health Association. https://secured.nmha.org/substance/women_disparities.cfm. Accessed July 3, 2009.

Cornelius, Llewellyn, Pamela L. Smith, and Gaynell M. Simpson. "What Factors Hinder Women of Color from Obtaining Preventive Health Care?" *American Journal of Public Health*, 92.4, 2002, pp. 535–539.

Costello, Daniel. "After the Diagnosis: African American Women with HIV Find They Must Also Endure Social Stigma." *Los Angeles Times,* December 6, 2004, pp. F1, 5.

Faber, Daniel. *Capitalizing on Environmental Injustice: The Polluter-Industrial Complex in the Age of Globalization*. New York: Rowman and Littlefield, 2008.

Gipson, L. Michael, and Angela Frasier. "Young Women of Color and Their Risk for HIV and Other STIs." Advocates for Youth, November 2003. www.advocatesforyouth.org/index.php?option=com_content&task=view&id=551&Itemid=177. Accessed July 3, 2009.

"Health Insurance Coverage." Washington, DC: National Coalition on Health Care. www.nchc.org/facts/coverage.shtml. Accessed July 3, 2009.

"HIV/AIDS Among Women of Color." APA Public Interest Policy Office, January 19, 2006. www.apa.org/ppo/hivaids/briefsheet2.html. Accessed July 3, 2009.

"Illicit Drug Use Among Hispanic Females." *The National Household Survey on Drug Abuse (NHSDA)*. SAMSA, November 1, 2002. www.oas.samhsa.gov/2k2/latinaDU.htm. Accessed July 3, 2009.

Luna, Stella. "HIV and Me: The Chicana Version." In Daisy Hernández and Bushra Rehman, eds., *Colonize This! Young Women of Color on Today's Feminism*. New York: Seal, 2002, pp. 71–84.

Smith, Andrea. *Conquest: Sexual Violence and American Indian Genocide*. Cambridge, MA: South End, 2005.

"¡Soy Unica! ¡Soy Latina! Arrives in Miami." *SAMHSA News*, 10.4, 2002. www.samhsa.gov/SAMHSA_news/2002News/article11.htm. Accessed July 3, 2009.

Sze, Julie. *Noxious New York: The Racial Politics of Urban Health and Environmental Justice*. Cambridge, MA: Massachusetts Institute of Technology Press, 2007.

"U.S. Public Health Service Syphilis Study at Tuskegee." Centers for Disease Control and Prevention. www.cdc.gov/tuskegee/timeline.htm. Accessed July 3, 2009.

Watt, Amber. "She Flew Over the Cuckoo's Nest at CSULB." *Daily 49er,* March 3, 2008. www.daily49er.com/2.292/she-flew-over-the-cuckoo-s-nest-at-csulb-1.90938. Accessed July 3, 2009.

Wong, Kristina. Kristina Wong. www.kristinawong.com. Accessed July 3, 2009.

———. *Wong Flew Over the Cuckoo's Nest*. 2008.

Prison: Bending Back the Bars

"Abuse of Women in Custody: Sexual Misconduct and Shackling of Pregnant Women." Amnesty International. www.amnestyusa.org/women/custody/abuseincustody.html. Accessed July 3, 2009.

Banks, Cyndi. *Women in Prison: A Reference Handbook.* Santa Barbara, CA: ABC-CLIO, 2003.

Cooley, Steve. "Three Strikes Must Be Reformed Statewide." *Sacramento Bee,* February 26, 2006. da.co.la.ca.us/pdf/3strikescooleysacbee.pdf. Accessed July 3, 2009.

Franklin, Cortney A., Noelle E. Fearn, and Travis W. Franklin. "HIV/AIDS Among Female Prison Inmates: A Public Health Concern." *Californian Journal of Health Promotion,* 3.2, 2005, pp. 99–112.

Harden, Judy, and Mary Field Belenky. "The Vermont Women's Prison Project." Women and Prison: A Site for Resistance. http://womenandprison.org/prison-industrial -complex/harden-belenky.html. Accessed July 3, 2009.

Harrison, Paige M., and Allen J. Beck. "Prisoners in 2005." *U.S. Department of Justice Bureau of Justice Statistics Bulletin.* November 2006, NCJ 215092. www.ojp.usdoj .gov/bjs/pub/pdf/p05.pdf. Accessed July 3, 2009.

Krikorian, Greg. "Three-Strike Law Has Little Effect, Study Says." *Los Angeles Times,* March 5, 2004, p. B1.

Langan, Patrick A., and David J. Levin. "Recidivism of Prisoners Released in 1994." *U.S. Department of Justice Bureau of Justice Statistics Special Report.* June 2002, NCJ 193427. www.ojp.usdoj.gov/bjs/pub/pdf/rpr94.pdf. Accessed July 3, 2009.

Law, Victoria. *Resistance Behind Bars: The Struggles of Incarcerated Women.* Oakland, CA: PM, 2009.

Levine, Susan. "Female Inmates Show High Rate of HIV." *The Washington Post,* August 2, 2007, p. DZ08.

"Marymount Manhattan College Degree Program for Women at Bedford Hills Correctional Facility." www.youtube.com/watch?v=9AmYT8TH7nQ. Accessed July 3, 2009.

Roth, Rachel. "Reproductive Rights in Theory and Practice: The Meaning of *Roe V. Wade* for Women in Prison." Center for American Progress, January 20, 2006. Reprinted at www.womenandprison.org/prison-industrial-complex/roth-1.html.

Schwartzapfel, Beth. "Lullabies Behind Bars." *Ms.,* Fall 2008. www.msmagazine.com /Fall2008/LullabiesBehindBars.asp. Accessed July 3, 2009.

Seidel, Jeff. "Sexual Assaults on Female Inmates Went Unheeded." *Detroit Free Press,* January 4, 2009. http://realcostofprisons.org/blog/archives/women_and_children /index.html. Accessed July 3, 2009.

Sudbury, Julia. "Gender Violence and the Prison Industrial Complex: Interpersonal and State Violence Against Women of Color." In Natalie J. Sokoloff, Christina Pratt, and Beth E. Richie, eds., *Domestic Violence at the Margins: Readings on Race, Class, Gender, and Culture.* New Brunswick, NJ: Rutgers University, 2005, pp. 102–114.

Women Behind Bars Project. www.womenbehindbars.org. Accessed July 3, 2009.

Reproductive Rights: Expanding the Options

Bridges, Emily. "HIV and Young American Indian/Alaska Native Women." Advocates for Youth. February 2007. www.advocatesforyouth.org/about/index.php?option=com_co ntent&task=view&id=439&Itemid=177. Accessed July 3, 2009.

Brodeurk, Paul. "School-Based Health Clinics." *To Improve Health and Health Care* (vol. 3). The Robert Wood Johnson Foundation Anthology, 2000. www.rwjf.org/files /publications/books/2000/chapter_01.html. Accessed July 3, 2009.

Davis, Angela Y. *Women, Race and Class.* New York: Random House, 1981.

Gipson, L. Michael, and Angela Frasier. "Young Women of Color and Their Risk for HIV and Other STIs." Advocates for Youth, November 2003. www.advocatesforyouth.org /index.php?option=com_content&task=view&id=551&Itemid=177. Accessed July 3, 2009.

Gutiérrez, Elena R. "We Will No Longer Be Silent or Invisible: Latinas Organizing for Reproductive Justice." In Jael Miriam Silliman, et al., *Undivided Rights: Women of Color Organize for Reproductive Justice.* Cambridge, MA: South End, 2004, pp. 215-239.

Image Archive on the American Eugenics Movement. www.eugenicsarchive.org/eugenics. Accessed July 3, 2009.

Krugman, Paul. "Republicans and Race." *New York Times,* November 19, 2007, p. A23.

"Media's Glowing Reports on Bush's AIDS-Relief Program Ignore Criticism by the Officials Responsible for Implementing It." *Media Matters for America,* December 3, 2008. http://mediamatters.org/research/200812030018. Accessed August 24, 2009.

"Media Matters Exposes Bennett: "[Y]ou Could Abort Every Black Baby in This Country, and Your Crime Rate Would Go Down." *Media Matters for America,* September 28, 2005. http://mediamatters.org/mmtv/200509280006. Accessed August 24, 2009.

National Latina Institute for Reproductive Health. www.latinainstitute.org. Accessed July 3, 2009.

Olson, Aileen. "CSHC Spotlight on San Fernando High School Teen Health Center." *California Schools Health Centers Spotlight eNewsletter,* June 2008, p. 3. www .schoolhealthcenters.org. Accessed July 3, 2009.

Pettypiece, Shannon. "Teens Having More Sex and Using Fewer Condoms, U.S. Study Says." *Bloomberg.com,* June 4, 2008. www.bloomberg.com/apps/news?pid=20601124 &sid=aRM2TuCBiqJI&refer=home. Accessed July 6, 2009.

"Public Funding for Abortion." American Civil Liberties Union. July 21, 2004. www .aclu.org/reproductiverights/lowincome/16393res20040721.html. Accessed July 6, 2009.

Silliman, Jael Miriam, et al. *Undivided Rights: Women of Color Organize for Reproductive Justice.* Cambridge, MA: South End, 2004.

Soohoo, Cynthia, and Katrina Anderson. "The American Health Care System Is Failing Women of Color." *AlterNet.org,* March 11, 2008. www.alternet.org /healthwellness/79211. Accessed July 6, 2009.

Tapper, Jake. "William Bennett Defends Comment on Abortion and Crime." *ABC News,* September 29, 2005. http://abcnews.go.com/WNT/Politics/Story?id=1171385&page=1. Accessed July 6, 2009.

"Uganda: 'Abstinence-Only' Programs Hijack AIDS Success Story." Human Rights Watch, March 29, 2005. www.hrw.org/en/news/2005/03/29/uganda-abstinence -only-programs-hijack-aids-success-story. Accessed July 6, 2009.

"'Welfare Queen' Becomes Issue in Reagan Campaign." *New York Times,* February 15, 1976, p. 51.

Mothers of East Los Angeles
Garcia, Lupe. "Aurora Castillo." In Susan Ware, ed., *Notable American Women: A Biographical Dictionary.* Cambridge, MA: Harvard University, 2004, pp. 107–108.
Mothers of East LA. www.mothersofeastla.com. Accessed July 6, 2009.
Pardo, Mary. "Mexican American Women Grassroots Community Activists: 'Mothers of East Los Angeles.'" *Frontiers: A Journal of Women Studies,* 11.1, 1990, pp. 1–7.

INCITE! Women Against Violence
De Leon, Celina R. "Unraveling the Violence . . . On Revolutionary Terms: An Interview with INCITE's Andrea J. Ritchie." *make/shift: feminisms in motion,* 2, 2007–2008, pp. 20–22.
INCITE! Women of Color Against Violence. www.incite-national.org. Accessed July 6, 2009.
Sussman, Max. "INCITE! Women of Color Against Violence: An Interview with Co-Founders Nadine Naber and Andrea Smith." *Critical Moment,* 22, 2007, [n.p.].

The Relf Sisters
Davis, Angela Y. *Women, Race and Class.* New York: Random House, 1981.
"Relf v. Weinberger." Southern Poverty Law Center. www.splcenter.org/legal/docket/files.jsp?cdrID=59&sortID=. Accessed July 6, 2009.
Volscho, Thomas. "Sterilization and Women of Color." *Racism Review.com,* September 22, 2007. www.racismreview.com/blog/2007/09/22/sterilization-and-women-of-color. Accessed July 6, 2009.

Chapter 4
Angry Little Girls! www.angrylittlegirls.com. Accessed July 6, 2009.
"Interview with Lela Lee: Creator of Angry Little Asian Girl and Angry Little Girls." *indieRag.com,* June 8, 2001. www.indierag.com/content/interviews/010606lelalee.html. Accessed July 6, 2009.
Noguchi, Irene. "'Asian Girl': Comic Strip of a Different Stripe." *Washington Post,* August 27, 2001, p. C01.

Politicizing Pop
Habell-Pallán, Michelle, and Mary Romero, eds. *Latino/a Popular Culture.* New York: New York University, 2002.
Hall, Stuart. "Notes on Deconstructing 'The Popular.'" In Raphael Samuel, ed., *People's History and Socialist Theory.* Boston: Routledge and K. Paul, 1981, pp. 227–240.

¡Soy Rasquache y Que!

Gaspar de Alba, Alicia. "Introduction, or, Welcome to the Closet of Barrio Popular Culture." In Alicia Gaspar de Alba, ed., *Velvet Barrios: Popular Culture and Chicana/o Sexualities*. New York: Palgrave Macmillan, 2003, pp. xix–xxviii.

Mesa-Bains, Amalia. "*Domesticana*: The Sensibility of Chicana *Rasquachismo*." In Gabriela F. Arredondo, et al., eds., *Chicana Feminisms: A Critical Reader*. Durham, NC: Duke University, pp. 298–315.

Pough, Gwendolyn D. *Check It While I Wreck It: Black Womanhood, Hip-Hop Culture, and the Public Sphere*. Boston: Northeastern University, 2004.

Trinh, T. Minh-ha. "Not You/Like You: Post-Colonial Women and the Interlocking Questions of Identity and Difference." In Gloria Anzaldúa, ed., *Making Face, Making Soul/Haciendo Caras: Creative and Critical Perspectives by Women of Color*. San Francisco: Aunt Lute, 1990, pp. 371–375.

Ybarra-Frausto, Tomás. "Notes from Losaida: A Foreword." In Alicia Gaspar de Alba, ed., *Velvet Barrios: Popular Culture and Chicana/o Sexualities*. New York: Palgrave Macmillan, 2003, pp. xv–xviii.

Zamora, Bernice. "So Not to Be Mottled." In Tey Diana Rebolledo and Eliana S. Rivero, eds., *Infinite Divisions: An Anthology of Chicana Literature*. Tucson: University of Arizona, 1993, p. 132.

Creating Rage

Carpenter, Cari. *Seeing Red: Anger, Sentimentality, and American Indians*. Columbus: Ohio State University, 2008.

Harjo, Joy. *She Had Some Horses*. New York: Thunder's Mouth, 1983.

I'm the One That I Want. Written by Margaret Cho. Directed by Lionel Coleman. Cho Taussig Productions, 2000.

Jones, Vanessa E. "The Angry Black Woman." *The Boston Globe*, April 20, 2004. www.boston.com/news/globe/living/articles/2004/04/20/the_angry_black_woman. Accessed July 6, 2009.

Lorde, Audre. "The Uses of Anger: Women Responding to Racism." In *Sister Outsider: Essays and Speeches*. Freedom, CA: The Crossing Press, 1984, pp. 124–133.

Notorious CHO. Written by Margaret Cho. Directed by Lorene Machado. Cho Taussig Productions, 2002.

Simone, Nina. "Mississippi Goddamn." *Nina Simone in Concert*. Philips Records, 1964.

"Strange Fruit." Independent Lens. www.pbs.org/independentlens/strangefruit/film.html. Accessed July 6, 2009.

Wong, Kristina. Big Bad Chinese Mama. www.bigbadchinesemama.com. Accessed July 6, 2009.

Yamada, Mitsuye. "Invisibility Is an Unnatural Disaster: Reflections of an Asian American Woman." In Cherríe Moraga and Gloria Anzaldúa, eds., *This Bridge Called My Back: Writings by Radical Women of Color* (2nd ed.) New York: Kitchen Table, 1983, pp. 35–40.

SOURCES 177

"Casualties of War"

"Anna May Wong." *Wikipedia.* http://en.wikipedia.org/wiki/Anna_May_Wong. Accessed July 6, 2009.

Beneath the Veil. Directed by Cassian Harrison. Independent Television News, 2001.

Mason, Richard. *The World of Suzie Wong.* London: Collins, 1957.

McMorris, Christine McCarthy. "Grappling with Islam: Bush and the Burqa." *Religion and the News,* 5.1, 2002. www.trincoll.edu/depts/csrpl/RINVol5No1/Bush%20burqa.htm. Accessed July 6, 2009.

Persepolis. Directed by Vicent Paronnaud and Marjane Satrapi. 2.4.7 Films, 2007.

Satrapi, Marjane. *The Complete Persepolis.* New York: Pantheon, 2003.

The World of Suzie Wong. Directed by Richard Quine. World Enterprises, 1960.

Publishing from the Margins

"Aunt Lute Books." www.lib.berkeley.edu/doemoff/womstu/fempress/auntlute.html. Accessed July 6, 2009.

Moraga, Cherríe, and Gloria Anzaldúa, eds. *This Bridge Called My Back: Radical Writings by Women of Color* (3rd ed.). Berkeley, CA: Third Woman, 2002 [Boston: Kitchen Table, 1981].

Smith, Barbara. "A Press of Our Own: Kitchen Table: Women of Color Press." *Frontiers: A Journal of Women Studies,* 10.3, 1989, pp. 11–13.

South End Press. www.southendpress.org/about. Accessed July 6, 2009.

"Third Woman Press." www.lib.berkeley.edu/doemoff/womstu/fempress/thirdwoman.html. Accessed July 6, 2009.

Bodily Expressions

"The Art of Kara Walker," Walker Art Center. http://learn.walkerart.org/karawalker?n=Main.HomePage. Accessed July 6, 2009.

Mendieta, Ana, and Gloria Moure. *Ana Mendieta.* Barcelona: Ediciones Poligrafa, 1996.

After the Earthquake / Despues del Terremoto. Directed by Lourdes Portillo and Nina Serrano. Xochitl, 1979. Released on video by the American Film Institute, 2003.

Rousseau, A. M. "The Empress Has No Clothes." www.amrousseau.com/articles/photometro10.html. Accessed July 6, 2009.

Señorita Extraviada. Directed by Lourdes Portillo. Women Make Movies, 2001.

Yarbro-Bejarano, Yvonne. "Laying It Bare: The Queer/Colored Body in Photography by Laura Aguilar." In Carla Trujillo, ed., *Living Chicana Theory.* Berkeley, CA: Third Woman, 2007, pp. 277–305.

Alma López's *Our Lady*

Calvo, Luz. "Art Comes for the Archbishop: The Semiotics of Contemporary Chicana Feminism and the Work of Alma Lopez." *Meridians: Feminism, Race, Transnationalism,* 5.1, 2004, pp. 201–224.

Latorre, Guisela. "Icons of Love and Devotion: Alma López's Art." *Feminist Studies,* 34.1–2, 2008, pp. 131–150. www.almalopez.net. Accessed July 6, 2009.

Tracy Chapman
Jackson, Jacquelyn L. "Tracy Chapman." In Jessie Carney Smith and Shirelle Phelps, eds., *Notable Black American Women.* Bonn, Germany: Verlag für die Deutsche Wirtschaft AG, 1996, pp. 88–90.

Pond, Steve. "On Her Own Terms." *Rolling Stone,* September 22, 1988, pp. 54–56.

Whiteley, Sheila. *Women and Popular Music: Sexuality, Identity, and Subjectivity.* London: Routledge, 2000.

Chapter 5
Here Is the Love

Anzaldúa, Gloria. *Borderlands/La Frontera: The New Mestiza.* San Francisco: Aunt Lute, 1987.

hooks, bell. *Sisters of the Yam: Black Women and Self-Recovery.* Boston: South End, 1993.

Jordan, June. "Where Is the Love?" In Gloria Anzaldúa, ed., *Making Face, Making Soul/ Haciendo Caras.* San Francisco: Aunt Lute, 1990, pp. 174–176.

Lorde, Audre. "Uses of the Erotic: The Erotic as Power." In *Sister Outsider: Essays and Speeches.* Freedom, CA: The Crossing, 1984, pp. 53–59.

Sandoval, Chela. *Methodology of the Oppressed.* Minneapolis: University of Minnesota, 2000.

Have Love, Will Travel

Lugones, Maria. "Playfulness, 'World'-Travelling, and Loving Perception." In Gloria Anzaldúa, ed., *Making Face, Making Soul/Haciendo Caras.* San Francisco: Aunt Lute, 1990, pp. 390–402.

To Know Me Is to Love Me

Ortega, Mariana. "Being Lovingly, Knowingly Ignorant: White Feminism and Women of Color." *Hypatia,* 21.3, 2006, pp. 56–74.

Smith, Barbara. "Racism and Women's Studies." In Gloria Anzaldúa, ed., *Making Face, Making Soul/Haciendo Caras.* San Francisco: Aunt Lute, 1990, pp. 25–28.

Loving Abroad

Ehrenreich, Barbara, and Arlie Russell Hochschild. "Introduction." In Barbara Ehrenreich and Arlie Russell Hochschild, eds., *Global Woman: Nannies, Maids, and Sex Workers in the New Economy.* New York: Henry Holt and Company, 2002, pp. 1–13.

Defining Worlds

Chowdhury, Elora Halim. "Locating Global Feminisms Elsewhere: Braiding US Women of Color and Transnational Feminisms." *Cultural Dynamics*, 21.1, 2009, pp. 51–78.

Kaplan, Caren, and Inderpal Grewal. "Transnational Practices and Interdisciplinary Feminist Scholarship: Reconfiguring Women's and Gender Studies." In Robyn Wiegman, ed., *Women's Studies on Its Own*. Durham, NC: Duke University, 2002, pp. 66–81.

Soto, Sandra. "Where in the Transnational World Are U.S. Women of Color?" In Elizabeth L. Kennedy and Agatha Beins, eds., *Women's Studies for the Future: Foundations, Interrogations, Politics*. New Brunswick, NJ: Rutgers University, 2005, pp. 111–124.

Future Lovers

Jamila, Shani. "Can I Get a Witness? Testimony from a Hip-Hop Feminist." In Daisy Hernández and Bushra Rehman, eds., *Colonize This! Young Women of Color on Today's Feminism*. New York: Seal, 2002, pp. 382–394.

Sarah Jones's "Revolution"

Mauro, Tony. "FCC Muffles Artist's Message." *USA Today*, February 24, 2003, p. 13A.

Parker, Lonnae O'Neal. "Battle Station in a Rap 'Revolution': Poet-Performer Takes On FCC for Ruling Her Feminist Song 'Indecent.'" *The Washington Post*, January 2, 2002, p. C01.

Sarah Jones. www.sarahjonesonline.com. Accessed July 6, 2009.

Women of Color Blogs

Ziegler, Kortney Ryan. "From Where I Sit: Academic Blogging as Intercultural Exchange." *On Campus with Women*. The Association of American Colleges and Universities. Vol. 36, No. 2. www.aacu.org/ocww/volume36_2/fromwhereisit.cfm?section=2. Accessed July 19, 2009.

INDEX

Gruber, James, 30
Gruver, Nancy, 139
Guardian, 128
Gurian, Michael, 34
gURL, 182–183
Guttmacher Institute, 71
gynecological exams, 67–68

H

Hahn, Jennifer, 193
hairstyling, 58
Halloween costumes, 60
Hardy Girls, Healthy Women, 114
harassment. *See* sexual harassment
Harvard Project on Women's Psychology and the Development of Girls, 26
Hays Office, 131
Headley, Justina Chen, 162–163
"Heat Wave", 155
Heelarious, 60
Helly Kitty, 15
Herkishnami, Komal, 152
Hernandez, Taizet, 151
Herold, Kara, 148
Heron, Cady, 105
heterosexism, 79–80
heterosexuality: breaking norms of, 77–79; cultural promotion of, 102; pressure to conform to, 59
high heels, for babies, 60
high-risk girls, helping, 190
high school, 62
Hispanic girls. *See* Latina girls
history, re-writing, 177
HIV, 196
home, leaving, 84
homophobia, 79
homosexuals. *See* LGBTQ community
homosocial bonds, 101–102
hooks, bell, 23, 96, 125
Hostile Hallways: The AAUW Survey on Sexual Harassment in America's Schools (AAUW), 87
housekeeping, 8, 10
How Sassy Changed My Life: A Love Letter to the Greatest Teen Magazine of All Time (Jesella and Meltzer), 138
How Schools Shortchange Girls: The AAUW Report, 17, 19, 20, 21

HUES, 138
hymens, 67–68

I

ideals, 93
identity: advertising as influencing, 128, 134–135; and intersectionality theory, 22–23; reconstructing, 164; scripting, 23
I Dream of Jeannie, 141
"Ignoring Diversity, Runways Fade to White" (Trebay), 128
imagination, 7, 8
In a Different Voice (Gilligan), 22, 23, 25
incarceration, of young women, 187–188
indirect aggression, 99
injustice, 121
In Love and in Danger: A Teen's Guide to Breaking Free of Abusive Relationships (Levy), 85
insults, 15
intellectual activity: conflicting messages about, 3; dumbing down, 116; lack of toys encouraging, 10
Internet resources, 82, 167, 179–184
intersectionality theory, 22, 37
intimacy: anger and, 99; nineteenth-century female, 101–102
I Was a Teenage Werewolf, 143

J

Jack, Dana Crowley, 95
jail, women in, 187–188
Jane, 138
Jayson, Sharon, 128–129
jealousy, 112
Jesella, Kara, 138
jewelry, 9–10
Jewish/Muslim activism, 190–191
Jorgensen, Christine, 78
Journal of Adolescent Health, 126
judgment, 62

K

Kearney, Mary Celeste, 146, 147–150, 173
Kelly, Christina, 137
Ken doll, 55
Kilbourne, Jean, 60, 130

politics, women in, 12, 185–186
popular culture: co-opting, 176; "pinup girls"
  in, 131; teen icons, 50, 133
popularity, 2, 6
pornography, 131
poverty, girls in, 24, 84, 196, 197
power: of assertiveness, 96, 140; female
  political, 12; gender and, 21; girl power, 134,
  159–160, 167; in growing female bodies, 65;
  as lost with age, 23–24; meanness and, 121,
  122; in post-revolution sexuality, 88–89;
  sexual games of, 86; vying for social, 104,
  106; in zine publication, 170
powerlessness, 82–83
Pratt, Jane, 138
pregnancy: education on, 73; school expulsion
  for, 192; teen, 72, 73–74
premarital sex, 69–70, 144, 146
princesses, 10, 11, 58
prostitution, 84, 196
psychological development, female, 26
puberty. *See* adolescence
purity: balls, 68–70; as denial of desire, 68;
  double standards of, 77; fathers as custodians
  of, 69; of "second" virginity, 70; of virginity,
  66–67
purses, 9–10

Q

Queen Bees and Wannabes (Wiseman), 59, 75

R

racial issues: and adolescent self-esteem,
  17–18; in beauty pageants, 52; in beauty
  standards, 63; in the classroom, 19, 20,
  32; compounded homophobia, 80; female
  behavior differences, 94–97; intersectionality
  theory, 22–23; models of color, 127–128;
  white pinup girls, 131; zines address, 178;
  see also African-American girls; girls of color;
  Latina girls; white girls
Racilicious, 162
RAINN (Rape, Abuse, and Incest National
  Network), 87
rape, 87, 113–114
reading, 33
Rebel Without a Cause, 143
Reel Grrrls, 149, 150

Reeves, Martha, 155
relationship: abusive, 82–88; demands of
  schoolyard, 108; in female psychology, 26;
  female relational aggression, 97–99, 103,
  104; online, 179
religion, 71
Renfrew Center, 10
resilience, fostering, 29
Ressler, Adrienne, 10
Reviving Ophelia (Pipher), 22, 23, 27–28, 120
Richards, Angela, 146, 148
Riot Grrrls, 156–160, 170
Roberts, Tomi-Ann, 129
Robinson, Matthew S., 76, 82
Robinson, Raven, 186
Rockettes, 49
Rock'N'Roll Camp for Girls, 159
Rogers, Annie, 26
Rosga, AnnJanett, 196

S

Sadker, Myra and David, 18, 20
safety, 86, 190
Sandler, Bernice, 191
"Sanitizing Puberty: The American Way to
  Menstruate" (Brumberg), 46
Sassy, 138
SAT scores, 33
Scarleteen.com, 82, 180
school: as denied to girls, 197–198; dropouts,
  24; gay-straight alliances in, 81–82; girls'
  loudness in, 94–95; high, 62; middle, 80,
  108; performance gaps in, 31–32; relational
  demands in, 108; resilience at, 115; sexual
  harassment in, 87–88; work, 18; *see also*
  education
"Schoolgirl Dreams" (Hahn), 191
*Schoolgirls: Young Women, Self-Esteem, and the
  Confidence Gap* (Orenstein), 22, 25
Schor, Juliet B., 7
Schwarzenegger, Arnold, 14
science: as discouraged for girls, 17, 18, 35;
  Expanding Your Horizons (EYH), 186–187;
  gender inequity in fields of, 19, 36; role
  models in fields of, 2–3
Scott, Elois, 20
*The Secret Lives of Girls: What Good Girls Really
  Do—Sex Play, Aggression, and Their Guilt*

ACKNOWLEDGMENTS

Much of what I do in life begins and ends with the power of love and inspiration that I receive from my *mami*, Maria de los Angeles Rojas Volio, and my *abuelita*, Lilia Lizano. In her own way, each has shown me what strength is and what courage means. Thank you also to my father, Herman Roberto Rojas, who always wanted girls. His belief in what I could accomplish is my guiding force.

My sister, Lizzy Rojas, is my best wish come true. I thank her for her infinite wisdom, selfless actions, and daily support. To my brother-in-law, Jonathan Wanagel, and niece, Annika, I owe much. Jon-Jay's wry humor and offhand suggestions have found their way into several parts of this book. Annika not only introduces the book's subject matter, she embodies what I hope ideally to express about women of color: passion, confidence, and the future.

My brother, Rigoberto González, reminds me well that siblings don't always have to share a bloodline. Thank you for your wit, loyalty, and unique friendship. Joyce White is similarly my cosmic sister and the voice of reason and compassion at all times. You know me better than I know myself.

Daisy Hernández, without you, this book would not have been possible. Thank you for your *amistad* and *comadrazgo*.

For providing me with validation, energizing my spirit, and illustrating every day what feminism is really about, I am forever indebted to Anna Sandoval, Barbara Kim, Eve Oishi, Linda España-Maram, and Rowena Robles.

To Tammy Ho, Amalia Cabezas, and Marisela Chávez, thanks so much for your insights and constructive comments. Our writing group has been a great source of comfort.

I am blessed to count on my long-standing friendships with Ricardo Soliz, Allyson Lazar, Liz Morin, and David Chen. Your supportive enthusiasm has always buoyed me. Likewise, thanks to Lupe García, Lakshmi Nair, and Diane Wade, who are all *hermanas* in solidarity.

I must also acknowledge two incredible women: community activist Sister Dominic and my former teacher, Frances Clause. Both were instrumental forces in my early life, and I owe much of my present success to their persistent care and commitment. My sincere appreciation and love to both.

Myriam Chancy, Cordelia Candelaria, and Vicki Ruiz have been integral in my development as a woman of color feminist scholar. They taught me to lead by example and have left me with much to live up to.

Jennie Goode is a gifted midwife. Her encouragement to "just keep going" is what ultimately birthed this project. I am also deeply appreciative of her genuine political commitment to the material—she *is* a sister-friend.

To my research assistant, Patricia Valladolid, who seemed to have dropped from the sky, many thanks. Her last-minute assistance was invaluable.

I have always received tremendous support from the National Association of Ethnic Studies (NAES). Thank you to my fellow board members, and especially to Cecily Hazelrigg-Hernández, Sandra Holstein, and Larry Estrada.

I also wish to thank CSULB's College of Liberal Arts for the TIP award, which provided me extra time to devote to this book. Similarly, my deepest appreciation to the many students I have taught at CSULB, especially those in my women's studies courses. I have learned so much from you and I hope this book offers some reflection of that.

Between the sentences and paragraphs of every chapter that I wrote for this book is the presence of my husband, Patrick Anton

Carlon Ontiveros, who offered editorial advice, took up more than his share of household duties, provided comforting words at the beginning and end of each writing day, and still other times, just listened. *Mil gracias,* love.

Finally, our pets, Nacho, Lola, Yoshi, and Muñeca, deserve special mention since it was they who most intimately witnessed my writing process. Their loving licks, cuddles, barks, and purrs offered the best distraction in the worst moments.

ABOUT THE AUTHOR

Maythee Rojas is an associate professor in women's, gender, and sexuality studies at California State University, Long Beach. She received her PhD in English from Arizona State University and her BA from Pomona College. Her research specializations include Chicana/o and Latina/o literature and  issues of race and sexuality. She is completing a manuscript on the uses of the erotic in Chicana literature, *Following the Flesh: Embodied Transgressions in Chicana Literature*. Her work has appeared in *Frontiers*, *MELUS*, *Women's Studies Quarterly*, and reference books such as *Notable American Women*, *Encyclopedia of Latino Popular Culture*, and *Latinas in the United States: A Historical Encyclopedia*. She also sits on the board of directors for the National Association of Ethnic Studies (NAES).

© Patrick Anton Carlon Ontiveros

CREDITS

Chapter 1

Two members of the Brown Berets photo was provided by and is reprinted with permission of Getty Images. © Getty Images/David Fenton

This Bridge Called My Back cover image (1999) is reprinted by permission of Cherríe Moraga and the estate of Gloria Anzaldúa.

Chapter 2

"Little Girl and Her Mammy" image was provided and is reprinted with permission of Corbis. © Corbis

"Cher Barbie" photo was provided by Terri Castaneda.

"Prostitutes in Vietnam" (1971) image was provided by and reprinted with permission of Magnum Photos. © Bruno Barbey/Magnum Photos

Chapter 3

Kristina Wong in "Wong Flew Over the Cuckoo's Nest" image was provided by Divine Eye Productions. © Antonia Kao/Divine Eye Productions

"California Three Strikes" image was provided by and reprinted with permission of AP Photo. © AP Photo/Damian Dovarganes

Chapter 4

The New Yorker Magazine, Cover, July 21, 2008. Drawing by Barry Blitt. © Condé Nast Publications

"Muslim woman in veil" photo was provided by and is reprinted with permission of Getty Images. © Getty Images/Christopher Furlong

Laura Aguilar self-portrait was provided by and is reprinted with permission of the Los Angeles County Museum of Art. © LACMA/ Laura Aguilar

Excerpted material from Bernice Zamora's "So Not to Be Mottled," from *Releasing Serpents*, by Bernice Zamora, is reprinted by permission of Bilingual Press/Editorial Bilingüe.

Chapter 5

Lyrics from Sarah Jones's song, "Your Revolution," on USSR: Life from the Other Side (by DJ Vadim), Ninja Tune, 1999 are used Third Side Music Inc

Selected Titles from Seal Press

For more than thirty years, Seal Press has published groundbreaking books. By women. For women. Visit our website at www.sealpress.com. Check out the Seal Press blog at www.sealpress.com/blog.

Colonize This!: Young Women of Color on Today's Feminism, edited by Daisy Hernández and Bushra Rehman. $16.95, 1-58005-067-0. An insight into a new generation of brilliant, outspoken women of color—how they are speaking to the concerns of a new feminism, and their place in it.

A History of U.S. Feminisms: Seal Studies, by Rory Dicker. $14.95, 1-58005-234-7. A concise introduction to feminism from the late 19th century through today.

Bento Box in the Heartland: My Japanese Girlhood in Whitebread America, by Linda Furiya. $15.95, 1-58005-191-X. A uniquely American story about girlhood, identity, assimilation—and the love of homemade food.

Hijas Americanas: Beauty, Body Image, and Growing Up Latina, by Rosie Molinary. $15.95, 1-58005-189-8. Reaching out to a growing "new majority," *Hijas Americanas* highlights for the first time the nuances, complexities, and challenges of Latina femininity, sexuality, beauty, and body image.

Shout Out: Women of Color Respond to Violence, by María Ochoa and Barbara K. Ige. $16.95, 1-58005-229-0. Women of color speak out on issues including rape, murder, slavery, domestic violence, poverty, and other forms of violence and oppression.

Girls' Studies: Seal Studies, by Elline Lipkin. $14.95, 1-58005-248-7. A look at the socialization of girls in today's society and the media's influence on gender norms, expectations, and body image.